SPORTS
JOURNALISM

SPORTS JOURNALISM

A PRACTICAL INTRODUCTION

PHIL ANDREWS

2ND EDITION

Los Angeles | London | New Delhi
Singapore | Washington DC

Los Angeles | London | New Delhi
Singapore | Washington DC

SAGE Publications Ltd
1 Oliver's Yard
55 City Road
London EC1Y 1SP

SAGE Publications Inc.
2455 Teller Road
Thousand Oaks, California 91320

SAGE Publications India Pvt Ltd
B 1/I 1 Mohan Cooperative Industrial Area
Mathura Road
New Delhi 110 044

SAGE Publications Asia-Pacific Pte Ltd
3 Church Street
#10-04 Samsung Hub
Singapore 049483

Editor: Mila Steele
Assistant editor: James Piper
Production editor: Imogen Roome
Marketing manager: Michael Ainsley
Cover design: Francis Kenney
Typeset by: C&M Digitals (P) Ltd, Chennai, India
Printed in Great Britain by Henry Ling Limited, at
the Dorset Press, Dorchester, DT1 1HD

Library of Congress Control Number: 2013932564

British Library Cataloguing in Publication data

A catalogue record for this book is available from
the British Library

MIX
Paper from
responsible sources
FSC
www.fsc.org FSC® C013985

ISBN 978-1-4462-5337-3
ISBN 978-1-4462-5338-0

Contents

Preface to the second edition

Since this book was first published in 2005, sports journalism and the media platforms which carry it have changed enormously. The digital age was still in its infancy then. It has since grown and developed, and the demands of sports fans have changed and grown with it. They now want information immediately and wherever they are.

Many major media organisations now encompass all journalistic disciplines – a newspaper, a website, television (online video) and radio station (podcasts) – and have a global reach. At the same time, the number of outlets for sports journalism has grown and fragmented. There are now many more websites devoted to sport, and the ceaseless flow of technological developments means fans can consume sport as it happens, wherever they are. More sporting events than ever are being covered live on television and radio. Newspapers cannot compete with that, and are no longer seen as the primary source of sports news, reports or interviews. To survive, they have had to find ways of adding value to the sports experience. They encourage their journalists to break stories on social media sites and use their own websites to provide added value. Journalists now also produce blogs, podcasts, webchats and analysis which can be delivered direct to mobile devices – a 'second screen' for those watching an event live or by broadcast relay. And they try to move the story on, and find the angles broadcasters will not touch because their relationship with the people they are covering can be too cosy.

Consequently, sports journalists must be able to operate across all platforms and disciplines. Print journalists are being trained in writing for the web and social media platforms, and to record audio and video clips for websites; web writers are learning radio and video skills; broadcast journalists are being trained in web writing and online video journalism; print sports editors are taking on the role of web editors.

At the same time, there has been a change in the relationship between journalists and their audiences. It is no longer a one-way process, in which journalists provide information and comment, and audiences consume it. Now, it has become a conversation. Online journalism (and increasingly all other forms of journalism) have become interactive, with audiences having the facility to comment on what journalists have done, and provide views of their own. Non-journalists have also become important sources of news and information, picking up stories which they either send direct to journalists they follow on social media sites, or post on those sites themselves. And sports professionals who take to social media sites to comment on the latest controversy become stories in their own right. Consequently, journalists must learn to navigate the very deep waters of such sites and pick out the small amounts of floating information which will be of use to them.

The field of sports public relations has continued to expand, with most major sporting organisations employing their own communications teams. Their websites have become an important form of income generation for them, and consequently sports PR professionals require the skills of sports journalists to service them. This trend has made relationships between journalists and sports organisations uneasy in some respects. Journalists feel sports PR practitioners have come between them and the managers, coaches, players and performers they want to talk to. There has been resistance on the part of some sports organisations to journalists filming press conferences because they want the material for their own websites; but sponsors continue to demand the widest possible publicity, so these tensions are being resolved, though it is a work in progress.

All of these developments are comprehensively covered in this new edition, which contains expanded sections on online journalism, broadcast sports journalism (especially commentary) and the role of news agencies and the work of freelance journalists.

But the principles of good sports journalism, which the first edition of this book has brought to the attention of students around the world, remain the same, as does the satisfaction of putting them into practice.

1

Introduction: the best job in the world?

It's the best job in the world, isn't it? Travelling the globe, watching the big sporting events for free from the best seats in the stadium, mingling with star players and athletes, seeing your byline in the newspapers or broadcasting to millions on radio or television, and being paid a lot of money for the privilege. That's the way many people see a sports writer's job. The reality can be rather different: hard and demanding work to tight deadlines; long and unsocial hours (most of them worked in the evenings or at weekends); a lot of time spent in research and preparation, acquiring the same depth of knowledge about the sports you cover as the most fanatical of your readers or listeners; earning the trust of a wide range of contacts among players, coaches and administrators; and the skill to write accurately and entertainingly at great speed and often under difficult conditions.

Nevertheless, there is no shortage of people willing to put up with all that for the undoubted rewards and satisfactions sports journalism brings. Jobs in the media, and in sports journalism in particular, are more avidly sought after than almost any other. Fortunately, the opportunities are expanding, too – though there will never be enough seats in press boxes to accommodate every aspiring sports journalist.

Sport is the fastest-growing sector in the British media, and the same applies in most other English-speaking countries. Not long ago, the exploits of muddied oafs and flannelled fools were confined to two or three pages at the back of newspapers, and to weekend afternoons on radio and television. Today, sports men and women are among the best-known and best-paid people on the planet. The world wants to read and hear about them, and the ranks of those who are paid to satisfy that demand are expanding accordingly. Sports people now feel the glare of the media spotlight more powerfully than almost anyone else in society. It's not unusual to find a hundred journalists covering a single match in English soccer's Premier League, and the jobs of national team managers are second in importance, in media terms, only to those of the head of state.

Sports coverage is vitally important to the health and prosperity of the print and broadcast media. The British newspaper market is the most competitive in the world, and increasingly, that competition takes place on the sports pages. From two or three pages at the back of the paper a few years ago, many national daily and Sunday newspapers have now expanded their sports coverage to daily, separate sections of up to 28 broadsheet pages – more space than they devote to general news or the arts.

In broadcasting, sport has spawned new radio stations in both the public and commercial sectors – BBC 5 Live and Talksport. It's also in the vanguard of the battle for television ratings. The rights to cover important sporting events are fiercely contested between both terrestrial and satellite or cable channels. The success of Sky TV as a satellite broadcaster has not been built on the first television run of feature films, as originally intended, but around its acquisition of the rights to cover major sporting events live. As a consequence, the demands of the broadcasters have reshaped the sporting calendar, fragmenting the traditional Saturday afternoon hegemony in soccer, encouraging day/night cricket matches and converting rugby league from a winter into a summer sport.

The growth of the internet has generated a huge variety of websites devoted to sport, operated by media organisations, sports clubs and organisations, and fans. This new technology also means job opportunities for sports journalists because it offers an extra source of income to the media by providing sports updates and reports on the web or by mobile phone. In addition to their websites, the biggest clubs now also have their own television channels, a trend that is likely to expand as more sports organisations wake up to the commercial possibilities.

It's not difficult to see why sport is so attractive to the media. They have the same number of pages and the same amount of airtime to fill no matter what is happening (or not happening) in the world, but hard news is an unpredictable commodity. What's more, stories generated by governments and politicians are often found boring by many people and, as the political parties huddle together in the middle ground for popular support, have lost their power to generate controversy and debate.

Sport is the exact opposite. It is predictable in the sense that the media know months in advance when the big events are going to happen; it has its own in-built excitement and drama, and a cast of stars. Hollywood should be so lucky.

The international sporting calendar goes from World Cups to Olympic Games to Test matches to Super Bowls to Grand Nationals and Boat Races without cease. Sport could have been invented for an industry selling a daily dose of sensation.

It could also have been devised as a ready-made source of material for those who enjoy writing. That is just as important an element in successful sports writing as enjoying sport. 'Sports writer', as the term suggests, is made up of two words – 'sports' and 'writer' – and to succeed you will need to be enthusiastic about both. It's not enough merely to enjoy football or athletics or racing: you must be able to convey your knowledge and enthusiasm to others in a lively and entertaining way, and to be willing to devote as much time to practising your writing skills as the sports people about whom you are writing spend practising theirs.

Sports journalism is a specialist form of writing, and it is broken down into narrower specialisms. The major sports, such as soccer, cricket, rugby, racing, golf, tennis and athletics, are usually covered by specialists in these fields. Why? Because fans know their sports and their teams inside out, and unless sports journalists want to look foolish and ill-informed, they need to be equally knowledgeable. Keeping abreast of the daily developments in a major sport is a full-time job. Only a few journalists are able to pick and choose the sports and events they cover. These are usually the brightest, wittiest or most incisive writers – columnists or feature writers with a roving brief to provide 'colour' pieces about the key moments in the world of sport.

But sports writing consists of more than just covering the big events. The media have space to fill, no matter what is going on, and they do so by whetting the appetites of their consumers with pieces building up to events, profiling the participants, and analysing performances, as well as with a steady flow of background news and features. And sport often bursts out of the sports pages when the activities of high-profile people hit the front pages or the top of the news bulletins, or cross over into other specialist areas such as fashion, business or medicine.

To cover sport successfully, you need to know the requirements of the medium for which you are working, and you need to understand the audience who will be consuming your work. Serious and popular newspapers and specialist sports magazines have unique styles, and sport is covered differently by print journalists and broadcasters. Radio demands a different set of skills from those of television, while internet journalism is a whole new ballgame. This book will help you to acquire those skills. The craft of the sports journalist can be learned. Indeed, beginners have a head start over those seeking to acquire almost any other skill. Many of us consume the work of professional sports journalists every day, and will have absorbed some of their skills unconsciously. What's more, the tools of the trade are cheap and readily to hand: pen and paper and access to radio, television and newspapers are all that is required.

The following chapters break down the job of the sports journalist into its component parts, and look in detail at every aspect of the skills required. They also offer exercises designed to help you internalise those skills and hone them to professional standards.

The book ends with advice on how to get started in a very competitive field. That is something which often demands great perseverance and a long apprenticeship. But if you're prepared for all this, sports journalism can be the best job in the world.

Context setting: media environments

Chapter Summary

- The media's influence on sport
- Sport's influence on the media
- Organisation and practice of sports departments and sports journalists
- Media markets and audience awareness
- Sport's cultural significance

Learning Objectives

- To understand the organisation and needs of the media
- To recognise the importance of sports journalism to the media's commercial success
- To identify the constraints within which media organisations operate in the sports market
- To understand what determines the sports agenda of news organisations in different markets
- To recognise how media audiences determine content and style

The media have an important and growing role in the culture of developed countries. As leisure time has expanded and access to radio, television and the internet has become almost universal, not only in the home but also in cars and in pubs, clubs, cafés and on the street, so the demand for material with which to fill the burgeoning number of media outlets has grown. The expansion of leisure has also led to an upsurge in public interest in sport, and a corresponding growth in the commercial success of major sports clubs and organisations. Manchester United, Real Madrid and the New York Yankees are no longer simply sports clubs but global brands.

If media organisations are to remain successful in an increasingly competitive market, they must reflect such movements in our culture and in the interests of their consumers. Indeed, the media not only reflect the culture in which they operate and the interests of their readers and viewers – they also help to form that culture and those interests.

THE MEDIA'S INFLUENCE ON SPORT

Much of the recent growth of interest in sport has been driven by the media, in particular satellite television, which has bought the rights to major sporting events and promoted them vigorously as one of the most effective ways of selling subscriptions to its services. To compete, terrestrial television (and radio) channels have had to follow suit. This has driven up the cost of media rights and vastly increased the income of sports clubs, governing bodies and professional sports men and women. It has been the major factor in turning many sports clubs into big businesses.

But the money television has put into sport has also given it the power to shape sports to its own ends. Beginning with the introduction by the Australian media mogul Kerry Packer of floodlit international cricket in the 1970s, television went on to fuel the massive growth of interest in soccer worldwide and the expansion of competitions like the European Champions League. It has even turned the traditions of some sports on their heads. Rugby league, a winter game in England for more than a century, has now become a summer sport, for the benefit of the broadcasters. Television has turned sport into a commodity and a sales tool.

SPORT'S INFLUENCE ON THE MEDIA

Media organisations have grown and adapted accordingly. New radio stations, television channels and websites have been set up devoted specifically to sport. They have developed radical new programmes such as sports phone-ins and rolling results services to attract and maintain viewers and listeners. They have also adapted the ways in which they deliver their content, to serve the ever-expanding range of mobile devices through which consumers now expect instant information. There has been a similar growth in specialist and lifestyle publications aimed at specific sections of the media audience, such as young men. They have carved out niche markets, either by covering sport in general or by devoting themselves to individual sports.

Newspapers throughout the developed world are devoting more and more space to sport. This is partly in response to the general upsurge of interest in sport, which is common to all socio-economic classes, and partly because newspapers recognise the influence of television on people's lives, and try to reflect it in their own coverage. The fact that multinational media organisations like Rupert Murdoch's International Media Group own both satellite television networks and newspapers, with their associated websites, has undoubtedly influenced the promotion of televised sport in those news-papers. And even those newspaper groups which do not have a stake in television have been forced to pay greater attention to televised sport because their readers subscribe to satellite television channels and have come to expect that service.

With the growth of the internet and the rapid development of devices capable of receiving online material wherever the user happens to be, the number of websites devoted to sport continues to expand. The task of making them profitable through advertising or by selling online services has proved more problematic, however. Many seek to fill their space with BLOGS and other material written by fans, the quality of which is variable, to say the least.

The best and most successful websites remain those operated by established media organisations such as the BBC, and by sports clubs and organisations which use the web as a marketing tool.

THE SPORTS DEPARTMENT

Sport is so important to media organisations that all but the smallest operate sports departments as part of their editorial teams, staffed by specialist sports journalists. In the newspaper sector, at both national and regional level, sport is one of the three traditional departments – news and features being the other two – which make up the editorial team.

The sports department is allocated its own section, either free-standing or at the back of the publication, and is responsible for filling its own pages. The department is nor-mally headed by a sports editor, who is responsible to the newspaper's editor, and who is expected to attend editorial conferences alongside the news and features editors, assist-ant editors and production executives.

The editorial conference determines the news agenda for the day and the space to be allocated to each department in the following day's paper. The number of pages allo-cated to sport tends to vary from day to day, depending on the day of the week and the sporting agenda on any given day. The sports editor must know what he or she intends to fill these pages with (normally a combination of news, match reports, features and opinion pieces) and who is going to provide the copy – staff reporters, freelances or agencies. Broadcast and online media follow similar patterns.

THE SPORTS TEAM

Most newspaper sports departments will have a relatively small team of staff journal-ists. In addition to the sports editor there will often be a chief sports writer, whose role is normally to provide a descriptive COLOUR PIECE on the major event of the day, and who will therefore cover a wide range of sports. There may also be two or three reporters covering the dominant sport in the area, such as soccer, and perhaps a reporter covering each of two or three other major sports, such as rugby union, cricket and horse racing. Some national newspapers will have reporters covering major sports like soccer based in specific cities or areas of the country so that they can build up close relationships with clubs and individuals in the area they cover.

Other leading sports, such as rugby league, golf, tennis and athletics, may be covered by FREELANCE reporters who have contracts with individual newspapers to supply daily coverage of their particular sport. A number of other freelances, some of them perhaps former professional sports people, may have contracts to provide opinion pieces or expert analysis. Many sports desks will rely on agencies for coverage of minority sports like hockey, ice hockey and basketball. And at weekends or for significant midweek sports programmes, STRINGERS will be asked to provide additional match reports.

The copy provided by these writers is normally handled by SUB-EDITORS. Their role is to check copy as it comes in for factual, spelling and grammatical errors, to make sure it fits the space allocated for it in the paper and to write headlines and picture captions. Some sub-editors may also be involved in page layout and design. The staff team of 'subs' will be supplemented at busy times, such as Saturday afternoons, when a great deal of sport takes place, by 'casual', freelance sub-editors. However, falling staff numbers are leading towards writers 'subbing' their own copy, cutting it to length to fit a template, and writing their own headlines.

WRITING STANDARDS

Sports writing once had the reputation of being clichéd prose churned out by lazy hacks. If such journalists ever existed, they would have difficulty getting a job today.

The quality of a newspaper's team of sports writers is a significant factor in maintaining audience share in a competitive market. The standard of writing in sports sections has risen enormously in recent years, so that it now bears comparison with the best of any other forms of journalism. This is as true at the popular end of the market as it is in the 'quality' press. Some forms of sports writing, such as the contributions of writers like Neville Cardus and Alan Ross on cricket, have a long and distinguished history. Now writers on other sports have caught up, and the best modern sports journalism is among the finest writing available anywhere.

RADIO, TELEVISION AND ONLINE

The sports team in a radio or television newsroom will operate in a similar way to that in a newspaper newsroom, although the number of staff will usually be smaller. The major difference between the broadcast and print media is that radio and television cover sporting events live. This not only calls for a different range of skills; it also means much more time and effort has to be devoted to organisation. A newspaper can cover a game by sending a journalist and possibly a photographer. Radio can often get away with a commentator and summariser. But live television coverage of a sporting event is a major operation. In addition to a commentator and summariser, journalists and sports professionals may be needed to provide expert analysis, and camera operators, technicians and a director are needed to provide and mix sound and pictures. The appropriate number of outside broadcast vehicles is also needed. Much of the time of producers and researchers working in television, who often work for companies set up to provide sports outside broadcasts, is spent in organising all this.

Online material is often provided by journalists writing for other PLATFORMS in the organisation, although it may be processed by a specialist team for the website.

FILLING SPACE

Journalists see themselves in many lights, from guardians of the truth and public watchdogs to entertainers and prose stylists, but the reality is much simpler than that. The basic task of any journalist is to fill space. Newspaper pages and radio and television bulletins have to be filled every day, no matter how many or how few significant events are happening in the world. Sport is a useful commodity for organisations which demand to be fed as regularly as the media because it is, in one sense at least, predictable.

We may not know when or where the next murder or terrorist outrage is going to happen, but we know well in advance exactly when and where sporting events will take place. We know they will provide the copy or pictures to fill a certain amount of space on a given day. Indeed, one of the reasons satellite television has restructured the sporting calendar is to make sure its schedules are always filled. Not all media organisations have the power to reorganise the sporting calendar to fit their needs, however.

Newspapers are the most demanding of all the media in terms of the quantity and range of sport they need to consume. But the cyclical nature of sport means that most of it tends to take place at weekends or on midweek evenings. There is rarely much live sport taking place on a Thursday, for instance, but newspapers still need to fill their pages on Friday mornings. To make sure they achieve this, they have to vary the type of sports story they carry according to the day of the week – the emphasis being on match reports after a busy weekend of activity, but with space for more news and features on 'slack' days.

EXERCISE

1 Collect a week's editions of your favourite newspaper, from Monday to Sunday (including a similar Sunday newspaper if there is no Sunday edition of your chosen paper). Analyse the content of the sports sections, paying particular attention to:

- the number of pages devoted to sport on each day of the week (some broadsheet newspapers run tabloid sports sections on certain days; count two tabloid pages as one broadsheet page)

- types of story – reports of events, pre-event pieces, news stories, features and profiles
- whether the proportion of each type of article varies according to the day of the week
- when you have collated the information, decide whether the day of the week influences the amount of space devoted to sport, and the types of piece used on any given day.

2 Look at the sporting calendar for the coming week. This can usually be found in the sports sections of Sunday newspapers. Try to decide how the fixtures and forthcoming events will affect the number of pages devoted to sport on each day, and how the proportions of reports of events, pre-event pieces, news stories, features and profiles are likely to vary day by day.

HANDLING COPY

Since hot-metal typesetting (in which each letter on the printed page was manufactured in newspaper composing rooms by printers sitting at vast machines, and headlines were set by hand from racks of metal type) was replaced by computer typesetting, the production of newspapers has undergone a radical change. Restrictive practices under which printers reset every word written by journalists before newspapers could be printed were swept away in the late twentieth century. Newspapers now operate with a fraction of the staff they once did, which is one of the reasons they can afford to increase the number of pages devoted to sport. One result of this is that the involvement of journalists in the physical production of newspapers has increased.

The typed (and sometimes hand-written) COPY, from which compositors set the printed columns of our newspapers, is now a thing of the past. The copy which journalists key into their computers is now what appears in the newspaper, but the process by which stories are tracked through the production system, and errors are kept to a minimum, has been largely carried over from the days of copy typed on paper.

Each story is given, by the journalist who writes it, a distinctive one-word CATCHLINE, so that there can be no confusion with other stories in the newspaper's system. Catchlines such as *match*, *race* or *winners*, should be avoided, as these names could refer to a number of events. Instead, specific catchlines such as *Bombaytest*, *Kentuckyderby* or *Olympichammer* should be used. This reduces the possibility of mistakes being made when stories are being collated on the sports desk and headlines or pictures attached to them.

The computer systems of many newspapers provide journalists with templates on which their copy should be written. These may have specific boxes for the journalist's BYLINE, the publication for which the piece is intended and the day on which it is scheduled to appear. Journalists FILING copy from outside the office, by LAPTOP, e-mail and occasionally still by telephone to a COPYTAKER, should include their byline at the top of the copy, followed by the name of the publication the piece is intended for and the intended date of publication.

Production DEADLINES dictate that sports reports are often filed in a number of TAKES (see Chapter 5), so the status of the copy (first take, second take or whatever) should also be indicated at the top of the story. If the story is incomplete, the words *more to come* or *more follows* should appear at the end of the copy. This is sometimes abbreviated to *mf*. At the end of a complete piece of copy, or at the end of the final take, the word *ends* should appear.

A writer's copy is usually processed by a sub-editor, who checks it for accuracy and length, before it appears in the newspaper. To avoid unnecessary queries, the writer should always ensure that unusual names or unusual spellings (Phillip instead of Philip, Macmillan instead of McMillan) are followed by the word (*correct*) in brackets. This tells the sub-editor that the name has been checked and the spelling is accurate. The sub will then remove the word (*correct*) before releasing the story for publication.

Most media organisations have STYLE BOOKS, which offer guidance on such matters as the preferred spelling of certain words, punctuation (especially the style for quotations and the use of exclamation marks), grammar, and how people and organisations should be described. They may also offer guidance on how issues like disabled people in sport, or racism, should be handled.

For ease of reading copy on screen, in-house computer systems will normally use basic typefaces like *Times* or *Ariel*. Journalists filing copy by laptop or e-mail should use similar typefaces.

Copy is then processed, cut to length, given a headline and placed in the appropriate page using a variety of computer software systems. It is at this stage that the typeface is changed to that used in the printed version of the newspaper. Pages will often have been designed in advance, with specific areas allocated to particular reports, although layouts can be changed if circumstances dictate it. A journalist's story does not become HARD COPY until the paper is printed.

There is a growing trend, however, driven by falling profit margins and smaller staffs, for writers to key their copy straight into templates, adjusting the length to fit the space available and writing the headline. This, of course, increases the responsibility on the writer for care and accuracy, as mistakes are unlikely be rectified by someone else further down the production process.

The broadcast media have their own dedicated systems for writing scripts and putting in such information as captions and the names of the reporter, newsreader and camera operator. However, every story in a broadcast news bulletin must also have a distinctive catchline, to make sure that the correct material is used at the right time. Spelling is less important to broadcasters (except in captions). Instead, they have to worry about pronunciation; and where mistakes can be made, scripts should offer guidance (see left) to the person who will be reading them (who will rarely be the writer).

> "The winner was ridden by John Cholmondeley (Chumlee) and owned by Mary Featherstonhaugh (Fanshaw)"

PRESENTATION

Journalists normally write their copy on word processors or laptop computers with horizontal, rectangular screens. The lines of copy that appear on their screens are similar in length to those in this book. The paragraphs are only a few lines long and there is plenty of white space, which makes the screen or the page easy on the eye and attractive to the reader.

But the people who will be consuming that copy – the readers of their newspapers – will be reading it in narrow columns. A paragraph of this length would be difficult to read in a newspaper because it would appear as a solid grey mass of type, with no white space. The type would be difficult to read and readers would be discouraged from picking their way through any more than the first few lines of any story because it would be so taxing on the eye. If every story were laid out in this way, the newspaper would be unreadable and it would quickly lose readers to other newspapers which laid out their pages in a more user-friendly way.

Copy written for newspapers should be broken up into short paragraphs.

A single sentence is often enough.

A newspaper paragraph should never be more than two sentences. These should be fairly short.

Copy presented in this way in narrow newspaper columns is much more friendly to the eye.

There is plenty of white space.

This makes it easier for the eye to navigate the text and avoid missing lines or reading the same lines twice.

But the length of paragraphs will vary between broadsheet (or serious) newspapers and tabloid (or popular) ones.

Short sentences, short paragraphs and short stories are especially important in tabloid newspapers.

They assume their readers will have a fairly low reading age.

The first paragraph of a story in a tabloid is often set in larger bold type.

The second paragraph will also often be set in larger type.

This format is another aid to easy reading. Sometimes, CROSSHEADS like the one below will be used.

EASY TO READ

Crossheads like these break the type up further.

They are an additional aid to guiding the reader through the story.

MEDIA MARKETS

Every newspaper is competing with many others in a fiercely competitive market. The way stories are laid out is one important factor in ensuring a newspaper is attractive to the readership at which it is aimed. Most media organisations exist to make money. Almost all of them are privately owned, and they have a responsibility to provide their shareholders with a decent return on their investments. To do that, they must attract readers, viewers and listeners.

Even those media organisations which operate in the public sector, like the BBC (British Broadcasting Corporation), ABC (Australian Broadcasting Corporation) or CBC (Canadian Broadcasting Corporation), must justify the licence fees or subsidies they receive from the public purse by ensuring that their product is as attractive to audiences as that produced by the private sector.

To succeed, they must be acutely aware of the market their product is aimed at. The products of the media are normally directed towards a specific sector of the market.

Newspaper markets

Mainstream newspapers are normally aimed at sections of the population that share particular characteristics. National newspapers, and those in big cities which have more than one newspaper, usually target a particular socio-economic sector of the population. They may belong to a particular 'class' (working class, middle class, professional), or share similar educational backgrounds, levels of income, age ranges or political allegiances.

Regional and local newspapers are usually aimed at the whole community. Their unique selling point is that they cover local issues (and in the case of sport, local teams and athletes) that other newspapers with a greater geographical spread cannot cover in the same detail, if at all.

These are, of course, generalisations, and the readership of particular newspapers is by no means limited to their target audiences. But it is useful (not least for the journalists who are writing the copy to fill them) to divide newspapers into the following categories.

Up-market

These are the serious newspapers at the top end of the market. They were formerly known as broadsheets because of the large size of their pages, though many have now adopted the smaller format. Their target audience is better-educated people in professional managerial jobs who have, therefore, reasonable levels of disposable income.

The sports which these newspapers choose to cover reflect the perceived interests of their readership. They give extensive coverage to the most popular sports in their circulation areas, but they also give greater weight than other newspapers to those sports which tend to be enjoyed by more affluent people, such as golf, tennis, squash or rowing.

Examples of such newspapers in Britain are *The Guardian, The Independent, The Daily Telegraph, The Times* and their Sunday versions (which in *The Guardian's* case is *The Observer*). Because the United Kingdom is a small country with a highly developed transport infrastructure, newspaper distribution is relatively quick and easy, and the newspaper market is dominated by national titles based in London. Sales of up-market newspapers, however, tend to be relatively low – typically less than half the sales of mid-market tabloids and well under a quarter of the circulations of the leading down-market tabloids.

In other countries, particularly those which span continents or subcontinents, newspapers tend to be city- or state-based. Examples of up-market newspapers in the United States include the *New York Times, Washington Post, Los Angeles Times* and *Chicago Tribune*. Australian versions include the Melbourne *Age* and *The Australian*, and in India, the *Times of India*.

Mid-market tabloids

These are aimed, as the name suggests, at readers in the middle to lower end of the socio-economic structure, with average levels of income and who have probably not been educated to degree level. They are usually old enough to have an interest in politics and economics, and to have outgrown the laddish frivolity of the down-market tabloids. Their content occupies the middle ground and is often aimed at the older end of the market. They sometimes also target women, on the assumption that many more affluent households will buy two daily newspapers – a serious one for the husband and a mid-market tabloid for his wife.

Sports coverage is also aimed at the middle ground, with the most popular sports again receiving the bulk of the coverage, but often with a slant towards sports enjoyed or played by older people with time on their hands, such as bowls or Test match cricket. Sports (or sporting events) that interest many women, such as Wimbledon or Ladies' Day at Ascot, may also attract extended coverage, often focused on peripheral activities such as fashion, rather than the sport itself. Two examples of mid-market tabloids are the London-based *Daily Express* and *Daily Mail*, and their Sunday stablemates.

Down-market tabloids

These are aimed at a working-class, and often youthful, audience. Because the majority of the population fall into one or other of these categories, the tabloids have the biggest sales. They tend to be brash and irreverent, with news values that place sex and celebrity ahead of more serious and important events. Their stories are usually short and sharp, often personality-based, written with the simple vocabulary and uncomplicated grammar that the least literate of their readers will understand.

Sport, therefore, with its high celebrity count, dramatic content and mass appeal, is a very important ingredient in the tabloids' recipe. Major sports stories will often be flagged up on the front page. The range of sports covered is heavily biased towards the most popular, such as soccer in Britain and Ireland, baseball and American football in the USA, cricket in India and Pakistan, cricket and the locally popular versions of football in

Australia, New Zealand and South Africa. This bias tends to be followed even when the most popular sports are out of season, with reporters seeking out fairly trivial news stories to satisfy the appetites of fans, often at the expense of those sports which are in season.

Typically working-class sports like boxing, darts, snooker and racing (often slanted towards betting) can also attract more coverage than they are given elsewhere. Sports with smaller followings may only be covered if an event is too big to be ignored, but because the tabloids tend to place a high value on patriotism, athletes and teams which do well on the international stage may suddenly find themselves at the centre of tabloid interest.

Examples of down-market tabloids are the *Mirror*, *Sun* and *Daily Star* in the United Kingdom – often referred to as 'red-tops' because of the striking colour of their mastheads – the *Daily Record* in Scotland, and the *New York Post* in the USA.

Regional and local

These newspapers cover specific geographical areas. In countries like Britain they are in competition with a strong and well-resourced national press, and rely for their appeal on their strong local coverage, not least of sport. In bigger countries, as we have seen above, almost all newspapers are regionally based. The broadsheet and tabloid newspapers produced in particular cities may have virtual monopolies, though even the continental countries have at least one national newspaper, like *USA Today* and *The Australian*.

The regional daily press in the United Kingdom has been contracting for many years, and although some cities, like Leeds, Liverpool and Birmingham, still produce both morning newspapers (more up-market and with strong national news content) and evening newspapers (middle of the road and heavily biased towards local news), most have just one title, now normally published fairly early in the day to give them more time on newsagents' shelves, but still referred to as an evening newspaper. These try to appeal across the socio-economic spectrum and are pitched somewhere between the mid-market and down-market tabloids.

Their sports coverage is overwhelmingly local, and their reporting unashamedly biased in favour of local athletes and teams. The most popular sports again dominate, but those with a strong local following – rugby league in the north of England, rugby union in the West Country, Aussie rules football in parts of Australia, hurling in Ireland, curling in Scotland – will also get plenty of coverage. Sports which have little following nationally will receive prominence if local athletes or teams are doing particularly well. The Sheffield *Star*, for instance, devotes a lot of space to ice hockey and basketball (neither of which are mainstream sports in England) because the Sheffield Steelers and Sheffield Sharks are leading British ice hockey and basketball teams.

Radio and television

Radio and television channels tend also to be pitched at different socio-economic segments of the population. They often use sport as a means of maximising their target audiences. The mainstream channels try to concentrate on the most popular sports – soccer in Britain and many other countries, American football, baseball and basketball in the USA, ice hockey in Canada, for instance. Those channels which are aimed at audiences higher up the socio-economic spectrum may choose to cover sports whose appeal is principally to that audience, such as rugby, golf or cricket.

The growth of satellite and cable broadcasting has led to a proliferation in the number of channels available, and to a narrowing of their focus. Many of them are devoted to specific types of programming, and sports channels are among the most popular.

This trend is closely linked, of course, to advertising, which is the media's main source of income. Advertisers tend to target niche markets, too – young men who drink beer, for example, or middle-aged women who buy washing powder. They know that certain sporting events can reach these markets in large numbers – almost any mainstream team sport attracts young men, while Wimbledon, gymnastics or show jumping attract women. One way advertisers have of predicting whether the media in which they advertise will attract their target audience is to look at the sports they cover and the space or time they devote to each. Sports like rugby league, boxing or baseball tend to appeal more to the blue-collar end of the market, while followers of golf, rugby union and tennis tend to be higher up the social ladder. A few sports, like soccer, appeal to all social classes.

EXERCISE: MEDIA ANALYSIS

One of the ways of differentiating the media is the way they handle specialist interests like sport. Take a selection of daily newspapers, including up-market, mid-market tabloids, down-market tabloids and regional titles. Analyse the content of the sports pages, making particular note of:

- the number of pages devoted to sport
- the choices of sports covered
- how the sports are covered – in-depth or personality-led
- style – how the pieces are written, use of language and metaphor
- type and length of story – match reports, news, features.

Having assembled your data, analyse how coverage varies between different sectors of the market. Ask yourself:

- Do the newspapers cover the same sports, and if not, why not?
- Do they do so in the same detail and at the same length?
- Is the emphasis personality- or fact-based?
- How do these things differ between serious papers and tabloids?
- How do regional newspapers fit into the equation?
- How does the language and structure vary? What does this say about the respective audiences?

WEBSITES

Almost all newspapers now have their own websites, which offer a similar range of material, aimed at similar markets, as the printed versions. Many also supplement this material with additional content, including video and audio clips, blogs and podcasts, and live, minute-by-minute coverage of sporting events. Because these are largely accessed on mobile devices, the audiences for them tend to be younger. This, in turn, influences the style in which they are written: the tone of such reports, even on the websites of upmarket publications, tends to be much more colloquial.

The influence of the web

Websites have had an important influence on television sports presentation. Although sports news channels and sports report and results programmes use live presenters or ANCHORS to deliver information, they also use tools and design features from websites to increase the amount of information they are able to deliver at any one time. Their screens now resemble websites, offering constantly changing information in CRAWLERS across the bottom, and frequently updated information in SIDEBARS. They are also heavily reliant on statistics such as fixtures, league tables and score updates.

The interactivity of websites is also being reflected in the broadcast media, by radio phone-ins and text and social media messages to radio and television programmes. The print media, too, now provide much more space for sports statistics, break up sports news stories and features with sidebars and graphics, use more pictures in more creative ways, and make extensive use of material gleaned from social media sites.

AUDIENCE AWARENESS

Because the national media target specific sections of the population, journalists working in it have to be aware of the level of education and income, and the range of interests, of their potential audiences. Regional newspaper, radio and television stations, on the other hand, tend to serve their entire communities, and the key distinguishing factor here is local interests.

Interest in sport is particularly susceptible to national, regional and socio-economic factors. Many modern sports were developed in Britain in the nineteenth century and have subsequently spread across the globe. With the exception of soccer, which has gained immense popularity among all classes and in most countries, the level of interest in the major sports tends to vary between countries and even regions, and between socio-economic classes.

In Australia, for instance, rugby league is the principal winter sport in some areas, rugby union in others and Australian rules football in others. In South Africa, rugby union is the dominant winter sport among the white population, but soccer is far more popular with blacks. In Britain, rugby union is popular in rural areas among the higher socio-economic groups, while rugby league is confined almost exclusively to the industrial areas of northern England, where it has a largely working-class following. In Australia and New Zealand, cricket is popular among all classes and age groups, whereas in England, county cricket tends to have followers of retirement age, while Test and one-day cricket have a much broader appeal. On the Indian sub-continent, cricket has a massive and passionate following among all sections of the community. The US and Canadian media, however, provide little space for any of these sports. The agenda there is dominated by indigenous games like gridiron football, ice hockey, baseball and basketball, none of which (except for baseball in Japan) has achieved the status of national sport elsewhere.

What most developed countries have in common is a growing interest in sport, particularly among men but also, increasingly, among women. Research carried out in Britain by the Newspaper Marketing Agency (NMA) showed that 54 per cent of tabloid newspaper readers turned to the sports pages first, while over a third of all broadsheet readers did the same. This figure rose to almost 70 per cent for tabloids and 61 per cent for broadsheet readers when those who scan the front page and then turn to the sports pages are included. Sport is also a major driver for users of websites and social media platforms.

What people read there is important to their daily lives. Sport is one of the most hotly debated subjects and raises more passions than most others. It also has a cast of celebrities whose activities are often of interest to people who have no real interest in sport. Consequently, many people read the sports pages for pleasure – relaxation and entertainment – as much as for information.

HORSES FOR COURSES

All of this, and the perceived correlation between an interest in certain sports and social rank, have significant implications for journalists. It determines not only the range of sports particular newspapers or broadcast organisations choose to cover, but the manner in which they cover them.

The choice of sports covered and the weight given to each of them will reflect the perceived preferences of their audiences. So will the style in which they are covered, from the length of individual articles to the choice of language and metaphor employed by the writers. Journalists writing for specialist journals will assume a high level of background knowledge from their readers, while those writing for general publications face the sometimes difficult task of providing audiences with all the information they need to understand the piece without 'talking down' to some readers. It is safe to assume that most people with an interest in sport in Britain will understand the basic rules of soccer and cricket, and people in other countries will have a similar understanding of their national sports. Minority sports will call for more explanation, and writers who specialise in them must avoid falling into the trap of expecting their readers to know as much as they do about the sport.

EXERCISE

Take a copy of a tabloid and broadsheet newspaper published on the same day. Compare their coverage of a sporting event, paying particular attention to the style in which the reports are written, their vocabulary and sentence and paragraph length. Then select another sports story from the tabloid and rewrite it in the style of the broadsheet. Compare your version with that in the broadsheet. Then take a broadsheet story, rewrite it for a tabloid, and compare your version with that in the tabloid newspaper.

SPORT'S CULTURAL SIGNIFICANCE

The cultural significance of sport goes wider than its importance to the leisure and media industries. In a shrinking world in which people have a high degree of social and geographical mobility, sport helps them maintain a sense of their local and national identities. While most of the population of Europe, for instance, are citizens of the European Union and share a common currency, they can cling to their roots through their local or national sports teams. Sports journalists help to establish and maintain this cultural significance. It tends to be expressed in their attitude towards the success or failure of the national teams, for instance, and sometimes in ways that are not healthy.

Peace may have broken out across the developed world, but international sport is often presented by the media as a perpetuation of old political rivalries, and even wars. This can often be detected in the language used by journalists when England are playing Germany at soccer, or India are playing Pakistan at cricket, or New Zealand are playing Australia at rugby.

HOW THE MEDIA DIFFER

It may seem blindingly obvious how radio, television, online and print media differ from each other, but it is worth trying to look beyond the obvious, because the specific characteristics of each medium play a large part in determining how journalists working for them operate.

Print

Producing a piece of print journalism is a relatively speedy process. The information needed to write most stories or features can be gathered over the telephone, from contacts or other sources, or collated from the internet, without the journalist having to leave the office. Although reporting sporting events ideally involves being there (print and online journalists do sometimes report some events from television coverage), the writing process is quick.

But production and distribution of a newspaper is a slow process, and it may be several hours, or even days, before the quickly produced copy is read, a factor the journalist should always bear in mind when writing. Print journalism is presented in a modular format within a single package (although there may be several sections within the package). The modular format means the reader can skip from story to story or page to page quickly and easily. This in turn influences the length and style of stories, which vary from full-page features to single paragraph news items. News stories are written to a formula which allows readers to absorb the main points quickly and abandon the story at any time they wish.

Radio

Although radio is often regarded as an instant medium, its news-gathering processes can be slower than those for print. Basic information can, of course, be gathered over the telephone, but putting interviews on air can take longer. Telephone interviews can be done quickly, but with a loss of sound quality, and for important stories it is often necessary for a journalist to go out with a microphone and recorder. For longer packages which require several interviews and 'actuality' sound (see Chapter 9), it can take several hours to gather the necessary material. This then has to be edited, usually by the same journalist, when he or she returns to the office.

Once a story has been assembled, transmission can be very quick – most radio stations run hourly news bulletins – or even instant. But radio is a linear medium. Unlike newspapers or websites, it is not possible for the consumer to move at will between items. It is imperative, therefore, that radio journalists hold the attention of their listeners, who have notoriously short attention spans, for the duration of a bulletin. That means keeping items fairly short – from about 20 seconds to a minute, with only the more important stories being allowed to run for longer than this. It also means cutting quickly between the various elements (voices and sounds) which make up the piece, before the listener becomes bored.

Television

Putting together a piece of television is a slow process, involving more time, effort and personnel than any other medium. Almost any piece of television journalism involves a camera crew, a reporter, and usually both, going out of the office and travelling, often long distances, to the scene of the story. They may already have spent a considerable time 'setting up' the story, making sure the people they need to interview and the things they want to film will be where they want them, when they want them. And when they get there, shooting even the simplest television story takes time. The editing process demands that sequences are shot from several angles, with CUTAWAYS to make editing easier. It can take an hour of shooting to produce a minute of television, with additional time needed for interviews.

And shooting the pictures is only the first stage in the process. A script then has to be written around the pictures, the voiceover track (if there is one) recorded, and the pictures edited into a coherent piece of television.

Transmission is also slower than radio because television channels tend to run fewer bulletins (although some satellite and cable channels now run continuous sports news programmes). Like radio, television is a linear medium, and the importance of holding the attention of the audience again dictates short, lively pieces.

Online

Websites can combine the techniques of print, radio and television (see Chapter 10) in a single package and in a largely modular form which can be instantly updated.

Perhaps the most important difference between print and broadcast media is in the behaviour of its consumers. If newspaper or website readers become bored with a story, they turn the page: if viewers or listeners become bored, they switch off or change channels. The channel changer is the ultimate critic of bad broadcast journalism, and more than in any other sphere of journalism, it is vital to grab the audience's attention and hold on to it. To do this, broadcast journalists must make full use of the extended and unique language that radio and television put at their disposal.

Table 2.1 Comparing the media

	Print	Radio	TV	Online
Medium	Words	Sound	Pictures	Mix
News gathering	Fast	Medium	Slow	Fast
Transmission	Slow	Fast	Medium	Instant
Style	Modular	Linear	Linear	Mix
Story length	Varies	Short/medium	Short	Varies
Format	Single package	Bulletins News show	Bulletins Magazine	Single package

CONCLUSION

The media are one of the easiest subjects to study because we all read newspapers and magazines, visit websites, use social media and see and hear television and radio every day. You would not be reading this book if that were not the case. Without the need to take time out from our normal activities, we can learn a great deal about how the media operate if we approach our daily consumption of the media actively rather than passively.

When you are listening to the radio, watching sport on television, accessing a website or reading the newspapers and specialist magazines, try to be aware of how specific media cater for different audiences. They all make different demands on their journalists, particularly of style. Study them carefully, and try to decide which market best suits your own style. Study the work of writers you admire and try to imitate them. There is nothing wrong with imitation as long as it does not extend to plagiarism, and a good writer's style will provide you with a useful template from which your own voice can develop.

A more analytical approach to your daily diet of sports journalism will help you to master the skills we shall be studying in the coming chapters more easily.

Summary

Sports journalism has expanded rapidly in recent years and is an important marketing tool for media organisations, especially satellite television and websites. Sport and the media have a symbiotic relationship. The sale of media rights has increased the income of many sports organisations and led to the increasing professionalisation and commercialisation of sport. In turn, the media have changed the way in which professional sport operates. Media organisations have specific processes for producing sports journalism and aiming it at specific audiences. The media help invest sport with certain types of cultural significance.

3

The sports desk

Chapter Summary

- The sports editor's role
- The diary
- Forward planning
- Prospects
- Processing copy

Learning Objectives

- To understand how a newspaper sports department is run
- To recognise the responsibilities of the sports editor
- To identify the roles of other key journalists
- To recognise the importance of forward planning
- To understand the newspaper production process

Because covering sport is a specialist job, most media organisations (as we have seen in Chapter 2) have dedicated sports departments which operate quasi-independently of the other editorial departments. The size of sports departments will vary according to the size of the organisation and the relative importance it attaches to sport.

The sports department is usually headed by a sports editor, who is a senior member of the organisation's editorial team, along with the news editor, features editor and possibly business, foreign, arts, fashion and other editors. Because of its self-contained nature, the sports department is responsible not only for reporting sporting events, but also for sports news and features and, in the case of newspapers, for page planning and the sub-editing of copy as it arrives in the office. It will also provide copy and other material for the paper's website and social media sites.

THE SPORTS EDITOR'S ROLE

The sports editor co-ordinates the work of the sports desk. With administrative help from a sports desk secretary, the sports editor is responsible for selecting the events to be covered by sports staff and freelances, allocating assignments to reporters, commissioning features, organising freelance contributors, selecting material from agency WIRES, page or bulletin planning, COPY TASTING, and making sure the sports department operates within budget.

The key to the smooth running of the sports desk is the DIARY. Contrary to popular belief, news (and sports news in particular) is rarely something which suddenly happens. Most of it can be carefully planned for. This is where the diary comes in. As well as the obvious lists of fixtures for a wide range of sports, the diary will contain details of numerous other events which will also generate sports stories: the meetings of governing bodies, disciplinary hearings, awards ceremonies, anniversaries of major sporting occasions and so on. Any story which is known about in advance is referred to as 'on-diary'. Stories which are not known about in advance – an athlete dying in a car crash or testing positive for a banned substance – are referred to as 'off-diary' stories.

The diary is also vital for the forward planning that is essential if the work of the sports desk is to run smoothly. Covering a major sporting event can be a complex logistical operation, requiring detailed organisation, such as making arrangements like media accreditation, travel and hotel bookings, and organising telephone lines.

FORWARD PLANNING

Although the sports editor is ultimately responsible for the content of the sports pages and the allocation of work to individual journalists, in practice this tends to be a much more democratic process. Other senior members of the sports team will have an input, and sports editors will be guided by the knowledge and wishes of their experts on particular sports. This is often done on an informal basis, but the formal planning forum is the sports desk conference.

The conference is the opportunity for specialist writers to make their bids for the events they would like to cover in the coming days and weeks, and to bargain for the space they believe their particular sports will need. The major sports will usually be allocated *some* space on the sports pages every day, and even out of season the most popular sports will often be given space. But the amount of space each sport gets, and the overall number of pages allocated to sport in the newspaper, will vary according to what is happening on each day. During events like a golf or tennis 'major', the Olympic Games or a World Championships in Athletics, extra space will be made available for what are usually minority sports, at the expense of the 'mainstream' sports. But there will always be an element of bidding for space between the representatives of the major disciplines.

The views of the chief sports writer will often play an important role in the way space is allocated. The chief sports writer is usually an experienced sports journalist with strong views and a distinctive writing style, who has a roving brief to cover whatever he or she chooses. This will often be the main event of the day. The result may be a COLOUR PIECE taking a detached view of the event, which means that a second journalist – usually the chief specialist in that particular sport – will also be sent to the event to write a conventional report. Indeed, at major events such as international games, a single newspaper may also send reporters to observe the event from the perspectives of both teams, and may even commission coaches or players from the competing sides to provide their after-match impressions. These will normally be 'ghost-written' by yet more reporters.

Staff writers specialising in each of the major sports will also make their bids for space, stating which events they intend to cover themselves and the ones for which they will need to hire freelance help. Contract reporters will also keep in regular touch with the sports editor, updating their schedules for the coming days and weeks.

Most sports desks will also call on the services of a number of journalists who are specialists in their own minority sports, such as snooker, hockey, ice hockey, basketball or bowls. They are usually freelances who may work for more than one organisation – a daily paper, a Sunday paper, a radio station and perhaps some television commentary work. They usually have excellent contacts with the governing bodies and players of minority sports, something no general staff sports reporter would have the time to cultivate. They may also cover other sports out of season.

The sports desk will also have access to copy and pictures produced by independent news agencies, some of which specialise in sport. The major agencies, such as the Press Association in Britain (see Chapter 11), provide copy to news organisations which subscribe to their services. It is available online and is constantly updated. The agencies provide sports news, reports of sports events, fixtures, previews, features and a results service. Smaller agencies operate in individual towns and cities and, as well as providing a general news service, specialise in the affairs of their local sports clubs. They accept orders to supply match reports to newspapers, broadcasters and online services.

Decisions have to be taken not only on which events are to be attended by the organisation's staff, but also which are to be previewed in the form of features or profiles of the leading participants. Sports journalists look back on the sport which happened yesterday, but in addition look forward to what is taking place today or later in the week. Previews are important not only to give audiences information on forthcoming sporting events, but also to fill space on days when there is not much sporting action. The sports supplements of Sunday newspapers, for example, will often contain almost as many features previewing forthcoming events as reports on the previous days' action.

The action that takes place on the sports field lends itself particularly well to photographs, and pictures play an important part in telling the story of an event. They are also vital to good page design. No sports editor, however, will have enough photographers to send to every event he or she wishes to cover. Although some newspapers employ a specialist staff sports photographer, many sports desks have to use general news photographers who will be assigned to cover sport at weekends or in the evenings. They rely heavily on agencies – some of them specialist sports photography agencies – for their pictures. They will also have access to a photographic library on which they can draw when a player or athlete does something particularly newsworthy.

One important aspect of forward planning is to make sure there will be enough material to fill the sports pages on quiet days when there are few events on which to report. This may involve previews of forthcoming events and profiles on the people who will be taking part in them; features on minority sports such as lacrosse, badminton or squash, which do not normally merit space; or 'timeless' features on sports issues which can be used to fill space on slack days.

EXERCISE

Analyse the content of a Sunday newspaper sports section, and make a list of the following:

- How many pages are devoted to reports of events that took place the previous day?
- How many of those events involved more than one journalist and what were their roles?
- What proportion of space is devoted to each sport? Is this determined by the importance of the events or the perceived interests of the paper's target audience, or both?
- What proportion of the section's content has been prepared in advance? What does it consist of – previews, regular columnists, profiles, fixture lists, fitness guides, sports equipment information?
- What is the contribution of the chief sports writer?
- Has the paper used the services of current or former sports stars and, if so, in what roles?

PROSPECTS

At the end of the sports desk conference, a set of PROSPECTS will be produced for each day of publication in the coming week. These are normally stored on the computer system so that all staff can have easy access to them.

The prospects (which some news organisations refer to as an ESTIMATE) for any given day will include a list of events to be covered, with starting times, the name of the journalist allocated to write the copy, and details of any action needed to organise accreditation, transport or telephones. There may also be an indication of the time the reporter's copy can be expected in the office. When allocating stories to journalists, the sports editor also needs to allow time for the writer to travel from one place on one day to another part of the country, or even a different country, on the next.

There will also be an estimate of which major sports news stories are likely to break that day, with details of expected timings of announcements, venues of press conferences, and some suggestions for follow-up stories if it seems appropriate.

There will be a list of previews and other features, with the names of the journalists from whom they have been commissioned, their length and when they are likely to be available, together with an indication of which regular columnists will appear on the day.

When the number of pages available to sport in an edition has been finalised, space will be allocated to each event to be covered in the form of a specific number of words. The journalist involved will be told how many words to write before the event begins. A typical day's prospects for an English national newspaper will look like this:

Sports prospects – Monday, January 26

Soccer: (FA Cup 4th round) Northampton v Manchester United (Jim Smith – 800 words), Manchester City v Tottenham Hotspur (Kate Smith – 650 words), Nottingham Forest v Sheffield United (Will Bennett – 550 words – 5.30 kick-off, late copy), Everton v Fulham (Louise Brown – 650 words), Wolverhampton Wanderers v West Ham (Martin Thompson – 600 words).

Saturday match follow-ups (early copy): (FA Cup) Arsenal v Middlesbrough (Jim Smith – 600 words), Birmingham City v AFC Wimbledon (Kate Smith – 500 words), Burnley v Gillingham (freelance – 450 words), Coventry City v Colchester (freelance – 450 words), Ipswich Town v Sunderland (Martin Thompson – 450 words), Liverpool v Newcastle United (Will Bennett – 550 words), Luton Town v Tranmere Rovers (freelance – 450 words), Portsmouth v Scunthorpe (freelance – 450 words), Alfreton v Chelsea (Louise Brown – 600 words), Swansea City v Preston North End (freelance – 450 words).

Championship: Derby County v Leeds (freelance – 450 words).

African Nations Cup: Congo v Guinea (James White in Tunis – 400 words – late copy).

Leagues 1 and 2, Scottish and Women's football round-ups: (Jill Green – 300 words each).

Rugby Union: (Heineken Cup) Exeter v Toulouse (freelance – 600 words), Sale v Biarritz (freelance – 600 words), Wasps v Calvino (Simon Charlesworth – 750 words), (National League) Bristol v Coventry (Dafydd Jones – 500 words).

Saturday follow-ups: Gwent v Leicester (Dafydd Jones – 500 words), Stade Français v Ulster (Mike Watts – 500 words), Harlequins v Brive (freelance – 400 words).

Tennis: (Australian Open) Andy Murray, Novak Djokovic and Maria Sharapova all playing (Marion Johnson in Melbourne – 750 words – early copy).

Snooker: (Welsh Open final) Ken Doherty v Ronnie O'Sullivan (Angus McKay in Cardiff – 400 words – ***very late copy***, result may only make final edition, or even hold over to Tuesday).

Rugby League: (Friendly) Bradford Bulls v Castleford Tigers (Eric Knowles – 350 words).

Golf: Dunhill Championship, South Africa (David Reilly – 750 words).

Rallying: Monte Carlo Rally (freelance – 450 words).

Boxing: Ricky Hatton v Vyacheslav Senchenko (Manchester – 750 words – late copy).

Racing: Leopardstown meeting (Sandie Scott – 600 words).

Cricket: (Triangular Series, Adelaide) Australia v India (freelance – 250 words).

Photographers: Caroline Harvey at Northampton Town; Tony Milligan at London Wasps; agency pictures from Australian Open, Leopardstown racing, boxing and Dunhill golf.

Colour pieces: Chief sports writer at Northampton/Man U (possible giant-killing).

Features: American football: preview of Super Bowl – 1500 words – Bill Fisher in Houston – copy received; Tennis: Profile of Aussie Open semi-finalist Victoria Azarenka – Marion Johnson in Melbourne – 750 words.

Columnists: Sue Jones – woman's eye view; Chris Coleman – sport on television.

News estimate: Soccer: Possible developments on Ferguson row with fans over transfers.

Cricket: Latest on England team for first Test in India.

Rugby Union: New Wales coach announced.

To fix: Press passes for Alfreton and Northampton matches; photographer's pass for Caroline Harvey at Northampton; rail ticket and connection times to Alfreton for Louise Brown; order Aussie cricket from agency.

WHAT THE PROSPECTS REVEAL

The events and sports the paper has chosen to cover reflect the interests of English readers generally and the readers of this newspaper in particular. Soccer is Britain's national sport and is followed by all sections of the community. The FA Cup, the oldest competition in the world, holds a special place in the hearts of English soccer followers and offers the possibility of high drama. Two of England's richest clubs, Manchester United and Chelsea, have been drawn to play minor teams, Northampton Town, who are a lower-league club, and Alfreton, who are not even members of the Football League. On such occasions sports journalists are always alive to the possibility of a 'giant-killing' story, and these two matches are given high priority.

But the fact that rugby union, golf and tennis – generally regarded as middle-class sports – are given substantial coverage suggests that these are the prospects of an upmarket, broadsheet newspaper.

Some of the choices and priorities are personality-led. The chief sports writer has chosen to go to watch Northampton v Manchester United not only because there is the chance of a shock result, but also because the United manager, Sir Alex Ferguson, is under pressure from fans over the club's transfer policy. Writing about both stories offers the prospect of an interesting colour piece, especially if United lose the match.

Similarly, a relatively minor snooker event like the final of the Welsh Open would probably not command much space in a broadsheet newspaper if it did not involve two former world champions. Notice, too, that because snooker matches tend to continue late into the evening, contingency plans have been made in case the result is not known before the paper goes to press.

You will have noticed that the important events involving the most successful and best-supported teams are covered by staff writers and allocated more space. Freelances are brought in for less important events and given less space.

The fact that most of the items in the sports prospects are fixed events means that pages can be planned in advance and specific space allocated for stories and pictures.

Prospects are a valuable working tool, the 'template' on which each day's sports coverage is based, although they are constantly being added to and amended. In the event of a spectacular story breaking, such as a stadium disaster or the resignation of a major international squad coach, they can be torn up.

CROSSING THE DIVIDE

Sports prospects are also shared with other departments at the main editorial conference, not only to keep the editor and others abreast of what the sports section will contain, but because sport now has such an important place in western culture that the biggest stories often break out of the sports pages and find a place in the general news section. Athletes who win Olympic gold medals, national teams which win world titles, local clubs which win national titles, the appointment or resignation of national team coaches and scandals involving prominent sports figures are deemed to be of interest to readers who do not normally follow sport. They are often flagged up on the general news pages, with a cross-reference to more in-depth coverage on the sports pages.

Such stories will often involve collaboration between sports writers and general news reporters. A sports writer will cover the event itself and the reaction of the sporting world; a general news reporter may be assigned to look at the national or local significance and report on the wider public reaction.

General news reporters and feature writers also keep an eye on the sports prospects because they often provide 'pegs' on which to hang related pieces in other sections of the paper. These pieces will often expand on the background to a particular element of a sports story; and because an essentially sporting story has crossed over into another area it is known as a CROSSOVER PIECE (see Chapter 8).

EXERCISE

This is a role-playing exercise in which a group of students can simulate the weekly sports desk conference. Someone should be appointed as sports editor, and some or all of the following roles should also be allocated (although these can be changed if other sports are more important in your own area).

- Chief sports writer

- Chief soccer writer

- Two soccer reporters

- Cricket writer

- Rugby union writer

- Rugby league writer

Decide which publication you are working for – up-market, mid-market tabloid, red-top tabloid or regional daily – as this will influence your decision-making. Find a list of sports fixtures for the following weekend. These can usually be found in the sports sections of Sunday newspapers. It should cover all the main domestic sports, and any major international fixtures which may be of interest to that newspaper's audience. Your task is to draw up the prospects for the following Sunday's paper, that is, reporting on the sport which takes place on the Saturday and previewing that scheduled to take place on the day of publication (Sunday), and perhaps important events later in the week.

In addition to the writers named above, you may call on a pool of contract writers who specialise in athletics, tennis, golf and boxing, although any of them can be asked to turn their hands to other minority sports. You also have the budget to employ ten freelance match reporters.

Each writer should scrutinise the fixtures and decide which event he or she wishes to cover. They should also consider which athletes, players or coaches they would like to interview for features previewing forthcoming events. They should then prepare to make a pitch for space in Sunday's paper and argue their corner against the other journalists round the table.

The sports editor should then give each team member the opportunity to argue for his or her selections, and for the space these will occupy. The final decision will rest with the sports editor, who must balance the conflicting demands of staff with his or her own list of priorities, which will be influenced by the perceived interests of the paper's readers.

When agreement has been reached, draw up a list of prospects for next Sunday's newspaper.

PROCESSING COPY

The purpose of drawing up a list of prospects is to make sure writers know where they are going, what to do when they get there and when to file copy. The best story in the world is worthless if it misses its deadline, and unless writers and reporters can do their jobs efficiently, the complex and pressurised operation that goes into producing a newspaper will not function. Most newspapers produce a number of editions each day, for distribution to various parts of their circulation areas. Unless copy flows into the sports desk at the times it is expected, the editions will either miss their deadlines (which may mean they cannot be distributed and the newspaper will lose money) or readers will receive an incomplete sports service.

But the writing and filing of copy is only the first stage in a tight and complex process. Once the copy arrives on the sports desk, time is of the essence, so as much work as possible must be done in advance.

Some of the copy destined for the sports pages, such as previews and features, some early-breaking news stories, fixture lists, columns and so on, can be processed well in advance of the newspaper's first edition deadline. Space will be allocated and sub-editors will correct the copy, cut it to length and write the headlines. Getting these pages away early clears the decks to concentrate on the hectic task of processing the reports from events as they start arriving in mid-afternoon (weekends) or mid-evening (midweek).

By this time, most of the writers will be out of the office at the events they are covering, but extra sub-editors, many of them casual workers, some of them brought across from the newspaper's general news operation, will have been drafted in to handle the flood of copy. Each sub-editor will be allocated a number of events or stories to handle.

To make sure that copy can be processed in time for the first edition, reporters will normally be asked to file their stories in a series of separate TAKES (see Chapter 5). The task of the sub-editors is to process the various takes of each story as they arrive, checking for factual errors and mistakes in spelling or grammar. They then assemble them into a complete story, trim it to the required length if necessary, and write the headline, making sure every story for which they are responsible is ready for the press by the first edition deadline.

They must then do the same with the rewritten reports that journalists file for subsequent editions. Complete pages are assembled on screen, with stories dropped into the space allocated to them as soon as the sub-editor has processed them. When a page is complete it is sent electronically to be made into a metal plate for the printing press. The late arrival of a single story can hold back an entire page and 'spare' stories are normally kept in reserve so that editions are not delayed if a piece of copy fails to appear.

Summary

The organisation of the sports content of a newspaper or bulletin is a complex process. The key role is played by the sports editor, who has the overall responsibility for the selection of events to be covered and for the allocation of personnel (both staff and freelance) to specific assignments. Sports journalists must be experts in their fields if they are to carry out their jobs effectively, and most specialise in a small number of sports. Copy is often written and processed to tight deadlines and a precise length.

4

Sources

Chapter Summary

- Contacts and contacts books
- Official information and press conferences
- Sponsors
- Wire services and news agencies
- Social media
- Other media
- The web as research tool
- Useful websites

Learning Objectives

- To understand how sports journalists source their information
- To recognise the importance of building up contacts
- To understand the difference between on-the-record and off-the-record information
- To identify official sources of information
- To understand the functions of social media in newsgathering and reporting
- To understand the role of wire services and websites
- To recognise the importance of using other media as sources

Journalists cannot operate without a constant supply of information. So where do they get it from?

One of the key skills of general news reporters is to be able to write authoritatively on any issue, whether they have any previous knowledge of that subject or not. But journalists who specialise must quickly build up an in-depth knowledge of their subjects, not least because their audiences – in this case sports fans – will often be extremely well-informed themselves.

Sports writers often come into the job with an extensive background knowledge because they have always been interested in sport. It may be a wide-ranging knowledge of sport in general, but most sports journalists specialise in particular areas. Some of them concentrate on one sport in winter and another in summer. Only the most highly regarded writers are given roving commissions to cover the entire sporting spectrum.

Journalists' own detailed, background knowledge of the sport they cover and the players and officials involved in it is often their most useful source. It enables them to anticipate stories and the likely reaction to them, and fill in background detail instantly from their own knowledge. It also means they know who to approach to substantiate a story and how to get hold of them quickly at any time of the day or night. But they also rely on a wide range of other sources, and the growth in the use of social media by both sports people and fans has added a new layer to the sports journalist's range of sources of information.

CONTACTS

Sports journalists must cultivate a range of CONTACTS – people within the sport who are willing to speak either on or off the record about themselves and other participants, coaches or officials, or about clubs or governing bodies. Many people are naturally suspicious of the media and the exposure they can give to a thoughtless or unwitting remark. Cultivating contacts therefore involves building up trust between the journalist and the informant, who will want to know that anything he or she says will be treated responsibly. In particular, contacts will want to feel comfortable that anything they say which is background information and not for publication will not appear in print or on air. It is therefore essential that both journalist and contact thoroughly understand what each means when they use the term OFF THE RECORD.

It is generally understood that when a journalist is given information ON THE RECORD it can be used in the media and attributed to the person who has supplied the inform-ation. All journalists will assume that people are talking to them on the record unless they are specifically told otherwise.

Off-the-record conversations can cause greater difficulty. When a journalist is told something off the record it means, strictly speaking, that it is for the journalist's inform-ation only, and should not be published. However, the term is sometimes used when the information can be used but must not be attributed to the person who has provided it. This is known as UNATTRIBUTABLE information. The practice is commonly used in political circles, where a system of 'lobby' briefings is used to inform journalists of government and opposition thinking. The officials who carry out the briefings are sometimes known as 'spin doctors'.

The practice is less commonly used in sport, although some athletes' agents, who want to place information in the media which might benefit their clients (such as a player's willingness to switch clubs), sometimes do so. Lobby-style briefings are also common in sports politics, especially where governing bodies from several countries may be bidding to stage a big event, such as the Olympic Games. Regular contacts will be well aware of the rules under which a conversation with a journalist is taking place, but in the early stages of a relationship it is essential to make sure that each side understands on what basis information is being provided.

Despite the suspicion with which journalists are viewed in some circles, building up an extensive list of contacts is not difficult. Many people are flattered to be courted by journalists and like to hear their voices on radio or see their names in print. Getting sport's biggest names to divulge their home telephone numbers to journalists is more difficult, however. The demands on their time from the media can be enormous, and unless you have built up a relationship with them while they were making their names, as many journalists do, the only way to make direct contact may be through their agents or their clubs.

CONTACTS BOOKS

Most journalists keep what used to be called a CONTACTS BOOK (although now it is more likely to be kept electronically, on a laptop or mobile phone). In it, they note the names, addresses, telephone numbers and e-mail addresses of people who have provided them with information. The same people are likely to be useful sources in the future. Journalists will keep in regular touch with the more important of them, ringing them for a chat or meeting for a drink. A good list of contacts gives a journalist the ability to speak quickly and frankly with the most senior figures in their sport, and increases the professional status of a sports journalist. It can lead to them being headhunted by other media organisations, with a consequent beneficial effect on their salaries. Some sports journalists build up such a good rapport with their contacts that senior figures in sport seek them out when they have something to say which needs careful handling.

CREDIBILITY AND AUTHORITY

The sources a journalist chooses or is able to quote will affect the credibility and authority of the pieces they produce. Quoting an unnamed source within a sports club does not have the same authority as quoting the coach or chief executive.

Similarly, the views of fans or supporters have more credibility if they seem to be representative of a wider group, such as a supporters' organisation or anti-racist group. The spokespeople for such groups can be useful contacts for sports journalists because they provide 'representation', whereas the views of individual fans are seen as being merely personal, though they can be useful if VOX POPS (see Chapter 9) are needed for a story. The views of fans' organisations and individual fans are now easily available on websites and social media sites.

OFFICIAL INFORMATION

Sports journalism is a two-way process. The media clearly need information to fill their pages and bulletins, but sporting organisations also need publicity to attract crowds to their events and to buy their merchandise. The best sort of publicity is free and the media have a vested interest in providing it for them.

Most professional sports clubs and bodies employ press or public relations officers (see Chapter 12) whose job it is to deal with media enquiries and ensure that a regular flow of information about their clubs and the individuals who work for them reaches the media. Although this may seem like media manipulation, the demand for media access is often so great that an organised response is the only sensible way of dealing with it. It also ensures equal access for all journalists.

The top clubs provide journalists with glossy media guides at the start of each season. Press officers supplement these with regular PRESS RELEASES about forthcoming events. These are now mostly sent by e-mail and are made available on WEBSITES. They will include information on players being transferred into or out of a club, injuries and suspensions to players, the coach's views on forthcoming matches, team selection, interviews with players, and post-match quotes and verdicts from coaches and key players. They may also deal with non-playing matters like ground improvements or redevelopments and ticket availability and prices. Most major clubs produce at least one press release a day, even in the closed season, to try to keep their activities regularly in the public eye.

This information is also made available – sometimes before it is officially released to the media – on club websites and social media sites. Indeed, sports organisations often choose to release information online first, to attract fans to their websites and to make sure that they set the agenda by writing the story from their own angle. These websites also include useful background information such as squad lists and career details of individual players, statistics, fixtures, directions for getting to the stadium and to away grounds, and a club history. Journalists should always check the websites of both clubs before covering a match: many of the fans will have done so and journalists should always know at least as much as their audiences.

Direct access to coaches and players is usually made available regularly to journalists, who have privileged access to club training grounds and are usually allowed to approach players after training sessions have ended. Coaches will normally hold PRESS CONFERENCES a couple of days before a match to answer questions and give details of injuries and team selection.

EXERCISES

1 *Sourcing information for a major sports event.* Select an event which is due to take place in the next couple of days. Visit the websites of the teams involved and gather information about team selection, injuries and suspensions, league positions and any

relevant quotes from players or officials about the forthcoming game. Write a 200-word 'preview' (see Chapter 5) of the event, based on the information you have gathered.

2 *Press conference role-play.* If you are part of a group, select someone to play the role of coach to a professional sports club. That person should visit the club website and gather the same sort of information as for the previous exercise. He or she should also be prepared to elaborate on that information in response to questions. (For the purpose of the exercise, it doesn't matter if this additional information is not strictly accurate.)

The other members of the group should prepare questions to ask the coach at the press conference. The coach should then make a brief opening statement about his or her team selection plans before asking for questions. You should try to ask questions that fill in the gaps left by previous questioners and that encourage the coach to give lively and useful quotes. Ask your questions in a friendly and encouraging manner. Avoid the temptation to be confrontational (which many people falsely believe to be the usual approach of journalists) unless the interviewee consistently refuses to answer an important question.

At the end of the press conference session, write up a preview piece of about 200 words as above, blending the coach's quotes into the story. The person who takes the role of coach should make feedback notes on the students' questions and the way in which they were asked.

SPONSORS

Another group of people keen to keep their names in the public eye are sponsors. Sponsorship plays a major role in the finances of most sports and is the main source of income in some. In return for putting money into clubs, individual athletes or organisations, sponsors expect to see their names on shirts and on the backdrops to photographic and television sessions. Many of them also spend a great deal of money and effort in making sure the sport with which they are associated receives the highest-possible profile, and this means making journalists' lives as easy as possible.

Companies which sponsor leagues, for instance, will provide journalists with detailed, pre-season press packs, often packaged in useful shoulder-bags which can be taken to matches. This is backed up with a weekly news and statistics service, made available to reporters in the press boxes of every venue at which games are staged, and sent to the sports desks of media organisations.

The sponsors of English soccer's Premier League, for instance, produce an information pack each Saturday which gives an overview of the weekend's matches. It also includes a full-page statistical preview of each game, full squad lists with the number of appearances made by each player, and goals scored by them. It contains the results of both clubs' recent matches, the results of games between the two clubs in the last few seasons, the cumulative history of matches between the two sides, and the leading scorers of each club. The statistics go into fine detail, such as the average number of goals scored and conceded per game by each club, the number of corners won per game, the average time at which they score or concede goals and the average number of shots on and off target per game. Goal scoring is scrutinised in minute detail, with analyses of how many are scored with the left foot, right foot or head, how many from open play, from crosses, corners, penalties, direct from free kicks or indirectly, and own goals. There are also lists of players who have had the most shots, the most on target, the most off target, assists, crosses, offsides, fouls and free kicks won.

The pack also includes team statistics and current form for each team in the Premiership, the records of referees in issuing red and yellow cards, a fixture and results grid for the league, the latest league table, a list of leading scorers, and details of how many games each club has gone since winning, losing, drawing, scoring or failing to score.

Even the most demanding journalist could not ask for more, yet all this is supplemented at the stadium by the home club's match-day programme, which contains the manager's comments, reports on recent matches, player profiles, injury updates, comment columns, club news, profiles of opposition players and more detailed statistics on both sides. Journalists are also given a team-sheet listing the players, substitutes and officials for the game. Some clubs also provide their own statistics and copies of press reports of their recent activities.

Sponsors of big one-off events like the Olympic Games have press teams based at the venues to supply a steady stream of information to the media (see Chapter 12). Those involved with mobile events, such as the *Tour de France* cycle race or Formula 1 motor racing, make complex arrangements for servicing the needs of huge numbers of journalists who are moving from town to town in pursuit of the race, or from country to country.

When there's a lull in the sporting action, sponsors will stage off-field publicity events, such as manager of the month awards, to which the media are invited.

WIRE SERVICES AND NEWS AGENCIES

Media organisations do not rely for all their information on their own staff or freelance journalists commissioned by them. Some of it is supplied by wire services or news agencies (see Chapter 11).

Wire services are so-called because their reports were originally sent over telegraph wires. They are now available to subscribers online. They are the means by which news agencies circulate their material.

Most big towns have news agencies which gather local news and sell it to national media outlets. They get much of their income from sport, covering the affairs of the teams and athletes in their areas in the same way a local newspaper would. They can provide a useful link between local primary sources such as clubs, and the regional and national media, who do not have the resources to cover all clubs adequately. News agencies filter out the parochial stories and highlight those of national interest.

Some sell their stories direct to the media, but others are channelled through national news agencies, such as the Press Association in Britain, which provide a comprehensive news, preview, fixtures and results service to their subscribers.

SOCIAL MEDIA

All these traditional sources of information have been supplemented in recent years by social media sites such as Facebook, Twitter, Google, YouTube and many others. Not only do people in the world of sport – athletes, players, coaches, owners, agents, administrators – use such sites to communicate with their fans and publicise their activities, but also fans use them to comment on events and performers, air their grievances about teams, clubs and coaches, and find stories and post pictures that journalists might never come across. Many organisations are now choosing to publicise their stories and events on social media sites, rather than using traditional publicity tools. And, of course, it gives journalists the opportunity to message sports people – many of whom may be otherwise difficult to contact – directly via their social media accounts.

In addition, journalists are now using these sites as supplementary – and often quicker – outlets for their work, and as a useful means of research. And social media sites allow journalists to talk direct to their audiences, and give their audiences the opportunity to talk to them. Sports journalists are gaining access to new stories, new sources and new conversations through social media. Such sites have become an important newsgathering resource as well as a powerful tool to reach and engage with new audiences. Social media skills are now essential to journalists.

Examples of stories which sharp-eyed journalists can pick up by monitoring such sites include: agents suggesting players may be unhappy at their current clubs and are looking to move elsewhere; players criticising other players or officials in the wake of controversial incidents; a fan spotting a new player arriving at a club's training ground, indicating that a transfer deal may be imminent; someone seeing (and perhaps photographing) two players fighting in a pub or bar during a night on the town; fans setting up protest groups to try to get rid of a coach, or even an owner. Sports journalists will typically follow all their local clubs and players on such sites. Players and coaches may react to a newsworthy incident through Twitter when they would not be willing to say the same thing direct to journalists. Message boards run by fans can also be a useful source of new stories, but these are often unreliable, so any information picked up from them should be carefully checked before use.

It goes without saying, of course, that the same standards – of both ethics and reliability – should be applied to information obtained from social media sites as from anywhere else. Hoaxes are common, and information from sources which are not known and reliable should always be verified by checking with the person or club involved.

No matter where a story breaks, there will always be members of the public with their camera-enabled mobile phones and access to social media sites who will provide almost instant information and pictures, even if no professional journalist is present. This not only allows newspapers and websites to use that material, but also gives broadcast journalists the opportunity to contact people at the scene via their social media accounts and interview them live while the incident is still happening. It is vital, therefore, that sports journalists know their way around social media sites, and get to grips with new ones as they are introduced, or they will be cut off from a huge resource of information and contacts.

This book is not the place for detailed instructions on how to use specific social media sites, not least because they are changing and developing very quickly. But as a general rule, the key is knowing how to reduce the vast amounts of information out there in the ether to manageable levels, by finding the right people to follow. This may involve limiting your areas of interest to a particular city or region, a specific sport or club, and following the posts of the key people involved, not forgetting the fans.

To make this easier, social media sites have devised a number of tools to allow you to put such people into groups and alert you to new posts by those you have chosen to follow, which saves journalists the trouble of constantly updating their searches. Understanding how to use the web and social media effectively is essential. But you need to become familiar with the most important digital tools and know when to use them. For instance:

Hootsuite can be used to create lists of the people whose posts you wish to follow.

Twitterfall.com is good for breaking news stories because it will give you lists of people tweeting about a specific story, and you can review those tweets to get a wide perspective.

RSS readers (Really Simple Syndication) allow you to search for what you are interested in, and subscribe to the appropriate blogs, websites and podcasts.

Google has a wide range of tools which will allow you to find the information you need quickly, allowing you to locate news, images and discussion boards, specifying particular locations or times, so that the information you get is always up to date.

Spend some time familiarising yourself with and trying out the various search tools offered by the most popular social media sites.

But social media sites are not simply sources of information for sports journalists. They also offer a fast and far-reaching platform for their work. No longer do journalists have to wait for the next edition of their newspaper or the next news bulletin to get their stories out. They can tweet the latest news direct from the stadium or the press conference, and in an incredibly competitive market, this is vital to stay ahead of your rivals. Fans now expect instant news, analysis and comment, and carry with them an ever-increasing range of mobile devices to allow them to receive it wherever they are. More than ever, the sports journalist's primary task is to be first with the story, to build up a following on a range of social media sites, and to use that platform to persuade followers to tune in to the sports bulletin, log on to the website or buy the newspaper to get in-depth coverage.

Many sports journalists have built up large followings on social media sites, where followers can enter into conversation with them, and where the news seems more personal. They can also put out requests for views or further information on stories. And social media sites provide a global platform for content, allowing fans who live in different countries or continents to keep abreast of their local teams. Social media sites are vital tools for reaching and converting new audiences, boosting newsgathering capabilities, and finding interviewees and contributors. They are also a useful method of quality control, allowing organisations to find out what people are saying about them and their journalists.

So important has social media become that major news organisations, like the BBC, have dedicated social media teams, who monitor and provide content for social media sites. Smaller media organisations will give the job to a specific individual, and some encourage all journalists to take responsibility for this area of their activities.

FANS

For every official club website, there may be dozens of websites and message boards set up by fans – the online equivalent of FANZINES. These are often of poor quality and dubious reliability and may contain libellous material but can provide a useful guide to what fans are thinking about controversial issues within sports organisations.

OTHER SOURCES

Most major sports have an established Year Book, usually published at the start of the season, which is a valuable source of records and statistics. The best known is probably *Wisden*, the cricketers' almanac, which has been recording the game's statistics for more than a century and which often becomes a source of news in its own right when it expresses its views on some aspect of the game in each new edition.

Fanzines and unofficial websites can be useful for assessing the mood of fans, particularly if a team is doing badly and a manager is under pressure.

Some sports journalists still prefer to keep their own records, although this is no longer essential because of the explosion in statistical information available from official and media sources.

OTHER MEDIA

Finally, the one source a journalist must never neglect is the media itself. The first indication of a big story will often come in a tweet by a fellow journalist, a radio or television interview, or as an 'exclusive' by a journalist on a particular newspaper. The media need to watch each other carefully if they are not to be left behind on a BREAKING STORY. Monitoring your rivals is a simple and easy way of keeping abreast of what is happening in the world of sport.

Sports journalists should read as many newspapers and specialist magazines as possible, and follow their rivals on social media sites. They should also listen to specialist sports radio channels, especially when travelling to cover events. News of team changes and injuries is often picked up first by radio journalists, who arrive at events well in advance of the start so that they can gather this information and use it as part of the build-up to their coverage.

Journalists should also resist the temptation to be choosy or snobbish about which newspapers they read. You may think the tabloids are sensationalist, but they often break stories first. This means that they play a major role in setting the sports agenda. The more serious newspapers and the broadcast media often follow up tabloid stories.

Conversely, you may think broadsheet newspapers are stuffy, but their coverage is often more in-depth and reliable. Radio and television stations can often be the first with stories, too. People involved in controversial events may be more willing to give interviews to the broadcast media because they know that what they say cannot be distorted.

The newsrooms of most media organisations have a full set of national and regional newspapers delivered to them every day so that they can check on the stories the 'opposition' have produced. Freelance sports journalists should always buy a couple of newspapers, and keep up to date with what is happening through specialist radio or television sports channels, sports websites and television text news services. Foreign sports news is usually accessible quickly through the websites of major newspapers in the countries concerned.

Letters to the editor in newspapers or radio phone-in programmes can also be a useful source of sports news stories, both nationally and locally. They can help journalists gauge the mood of fans, and give early warning of campaigns to oust managers or coaches, for instance.

MEDIA WEBSITES

The best sites are usually those set up by existing communications organisations such as newspapers and broadcasting companies. These include the BBC and *The Guardian* in Britain, the *New York Times* and *Washington Post* in the USA, the *Melbourne Age* and *The Australian* in Australia, the *Times of India* and many others. These sites provide not only alternative (and often free) access to material produced for the newspapers or broadcasters which own them, but also additional material produced specifically for their websites. This ranges from live minute-by-minute reports, breaking news, blogs, features, columns and statistics to chat rooms, podcasts and other interactive facilities and (an invaluable reference source for other journalists) access to much of the material they have published in previous months and years, which is known as the ARCHIVE.

They often employ specialist teams of journalists to service their websites, either writing their own copy from a variety of sources, or turning copy produced for print or broadcast into material suitable for online consumption.

The growth of the web has also spawned new companies specialising in online sports journalism. These sites sometimes cover a single sport, and sometimes range over many. They are usually funded by advertising, although some also offer subscription services.

THE WEB AS RESEARCH TOOL

Although there is a sense in which the internet has revolutionised publishing, it has complemented and influenced, rather than replaced, existing media. Because it offers instantly available information from a wide range of organisations that can be accessed from anywhere, one of its principal uses for journalists is as a research tool.

The easiest way to find information online is to use a search engine such as Google or Yahoo. Call up the home page, type your keyword or words into the search box, and let the search engine do the rest. It is advisable, however, to try to define your search as narrowly as possible, or the response may overwhelm you. A search for sites relating to popular organisations such as Manchester United or the New York Yankees may throw up pages of sites. In addition to many well-organised and informative sites, there is a lot of junk out there. One way of refining your search is to request only official sites; another is to choose to search for sites only in your own country, or in the country in which the organisation you are looking for is based, rather than worldwide. To get only current information, you can search by date.

Cutting and pasting information from the internet is easy, but it also presents hazards. Websites are covered by the same copyright legislation as printed or broadcast material, and you should beware of infringing that copyright (see Appendix 2). You should also be wary of plagiarism. You must not pass off someone else's work as your own, and neither should you let what someone else has written get in the way of producing your own distinctive piece of journalism in your own style. If you use information from anything other than a primary source, such as a club website or an individual athlete's own site, you need to check its accuracy just as you would from any other media source.

Researching a story on the net will often involve visiting more than one site to gather together the ingredients. For instance, if a player is rumoured to be moving from one club to another, the websites of the clubs involved will probably offer their official view on the story, and the player's own site or that of his agent may have something to say. Sometimes the information found there will be conflicting, but it can still form the basis for a story.

The internet has also made it more difficult for people to hide from journalists. There are times – for instance, if they have failed a drugs test or have been involved in some scandal away from the arena – when sports people would prefer to keep a low profile. The internet offers additional ways of tracking people down, through online telephone directories and easily searchable registers which will provide addresses in response to a search for a name. Journalists can, of course, also use e-mail or social media sites as ways of reaching someone for a quote when it is difficult to get a personal interview or reach them by phone. Most people read their e-mails and keep abreast of social media, and a reply takes only seconds. An e-mail interview can sometimes be useful, though it is no substitute for speaking to someone direct.

USEFUL WEBSITES

www.bbc.co.uk/sport provides the latest news on all major sports in Britain and world-wide, live reports, statistics and biographies of leading sports personalities.

Major broadcasting organisations in other countries, and leading newspapers like *The Guardian* in Britain, *The Australian* and the *New York Times*, also have good websites with a strong sports content. They are often free, although some may ask you to register and some charge for access.

Sports governing bodies and international federations usually have their own websites, many of them with links to leading clubs. Most major professional sports clubs and franchises also have their own sites, which are regularly updated with the latest news and have excellent statistical databases.

There are also comprehensive generic sites for many sports. Searching for the appropriate sport in a search engine like Google will find them.

Summary

Sports journalists rely on a variety of sources for their material. Many of them are specialists, and the most important source of information is their own experience and knowledge. They also need a wide range of contacts. Keeping names and telephone numbers in a contacts book helps them get hold of the people they need to talk to easily. Sports organisations and sponsors have a vested interest in keeping journalists well informed, and they provide a constant stream of material. News agencies, social media sites and websites are also useful resources, and all sports journalists depend on other media - especially the tweets of their fellow journalists - to keep themselves informed of the latest developments.

5 Interviewing

Chapter Summary

- Setting up an interview
- Establishing the rules
- Informal interviews
- The importance of research
- Interview technique
- Preparing questions
- Notebooks and recorders
- Writing up interviews
- Quoting fairly and accurately

Learning Objectives

- To understand the functions of a journalistic interview
- To be able to make satisfactory arrangements for conducting an interview
- To appreciate the value of research and the preparation of appropriate questions
- To understand how to select and use those parts of an interview which are appropriate to your needs
- To appreciate the importance of using quotes fairly and accurately

Sports journalism is not only about what performers do on the field of play, but what they and their coaches and administrators say off it. As with any other form of journalism, one of the most important skills is to be able to gain access to the people at the centre of the story, get them to give you their views and impressions, and present what they say clearly and accurately.

This will normally involve conducting an interview with the person or people involved, and selecting relevant quotes (and perhaps other pieces of information) for inclusion in the piece being prepared. As we shall see in later chapters, journalists writing features, news stories or match reports will be looking for certain kinds of information. Conducting a successful interview involves more than merely turning up with a notebook and asking the first questions which come into your head. A useful interview will involve careful preparation and a clear knowledge of what you hope it will produce. This chapter is designed to help you get the best from your interviews. (Broadcast interviews demand their own techniques, and they are dealt with more thoroughly in Chapter 9.)

SETTING UP THE INTERVIEW

The first task journalists face is to persuade prospective interviewees to talk to them. If you are setting up an interview direct with the interviewee, be polite and remember that at the precise moment you call they may have more important things to do than arrange to be interviewed by you. Explain why you want to do the interview, what the end product will be, where it is going to appear and how long the interview is likely to take. Anyone who is being asked to reveal details about their lives has a right to know these things, and if they are being asked to give up their time, they will want to know if it is going to be worthwhile.

That is not the same, however, as agreeing to allow the subject any kind of editorial control over the finished article. If they are worried about this, try to assure them what they say will be treated accurately and fairly, but resist any request to see the piece before publication. If there is no avoiding this, and getting the interview is sufficiently important, make it clear that the only changes you will be prepared to make are to errors of fact. Giving a subject the power of veto over the tone of an article or the views of the writer (or those of anyone else who is quoted in it) means that it can never be an objective piece. Some sports people (or their agents – see below) have begun asking journalists to sign written agreements giving them the right to make changes to a finished article. An interview conducted under these circumstances is rarely worth doing, and there are other ways (see below) of getting the quotes you need to write your piece.

Some interviews have to be arranged through an AGENT or press officer. Try to establish a good relationship with these people, as they are often the key to access. State which organisation you are working for, the purpose of the interview, where you would prefer to conduct the interview and whether you are taking a photographer with you. You may have to be prepared to fit into an athlete's tight schedule, so always try to give a duration for the interview. Somewhere between 30 minutes and an hour should be ample for all but the longest profile piece. You may have to make do with less, in which case preparation will become even more important (see below).

WHERE TO CONDUCT THE INTERVIEW

If you are offered the choice of venue for the interview, try to choose somewhere which will give you a better insight into the interviewee's personality, such as his or her home, or into his or her professional life, such as dressing room, training ground or stadium. People's surroundings always say something about them, and describing these surroundings in your piece will set the subject in context for the reader. You should also try to make sure that you will be free from interruptions and the presence of other people (unless you want comments from them as well) who might inhibit the interviewee's freedom to talk.

The venue you choose may depend on whether your piece is to be illustrated with pictures. The photographs will be more interesting if we see the athlete in his or her natural environment, and it is less demanding of an interviewee's time to take the photographs at the same time as the interview. It is good practice to liaise with your photographer before making the arrangements for the interview. The photographer may have a suggestion to make that you had not thought of, which could lead to a more interesting piece.

The choice of venue is particularly important for television interviews (see Chapter 9).

RULES OF ENGAGEMENT

It is essential to establish in advance the conditions under which an interview is to take place. Most interviews are straightforward and come with no preconditions. But some interviewees or their representatives may ask to see a list of questions before being interviewed, or state that some areas of questioning are off-limits. You will need to take a judgement on the legitimacy of such requests before deciding whether to go ahead with the interview. In either case, the spontaneity of the interview will be reduced, but there may be no harm in submitting questions.

The interview process itself should offer the opportunity of getting subjects to expand on their answers, and despite the best efforts of their representatives to protect them, once they come face to face with a journalist, subjects are often amenable to answering follow-up questions.

Whether or not to proceed if some areas are off-limits will depend on how central those areas are to the piece you are hoping to produce. You may choose to agree if the information you will be able to get by sticking to those areas which are on-limits is essential to your article. In any event, the fact that a subject is not prepared to answer questions on a particular issue should not prevent you from covering that issue in your piece, perhaps by using other sources to throw light on it. And the fact that the subject is not prepared to discuss the issue is revealing in itself.

Unless the organisation for which you are working is paying a fee for the interview (which does not happen very often), you should avoid allowing interviewees or their agents to see and approve your copy or broadcast tape. This is close to censorship, and if it means you don't get an interview, there are other ways of obtaining information.

INFORMAL INTERVIEWS

Leading sports personalities get so many requests for interviews that they cannot possibly agree to them all. Unless you are working for a major newspaper, magazine or broadcaster, your chances of getting a face-to-face or even telephone interview with the top performers or coaches may be slim. But that should not prevent you from writing your profile. Like celebrities in any field, the top sports stars can be elusive, but they usually have to make themselves available to the media at some point. They often have to attend press conferences after events in which they have taken part under the terms of the contract they have with the event organisers, whose interests are to keep the media happy. They also make public appearances, which usually include media opportunities of some sort, in support of sponsors who are paying them for the publicity they attract. Although not as satisfactory as a one-to-one interview, these appearances offer journalists another opportunity of asking questions.

As a last resort, you may have to get what you can where you can. This may involve talking to your subjects as they come out of the players' or competitors' entrance, in the stadium car park or at the training ground. This is sometimes known as an AMBUSH INTERVIEW, though it should not be treated as a licence to behave rudely or unethically. A certain amount of unwanted attention comes with the territory for highly paid sports people who make their living in the entertainment industry, but they should only be approached in the appropriate circumstances. Celebrities have a right to privacy, too, and it would not be appropriate to interrupt a family shopping trip or a meal in a restaurant to ask questions.

If you do decide to conduct an ambush interview, be polite but persistent, be very clear before you approach the subject about the questions you would like answers to, and be prepared to phrase them in a number of different ways. This can sometimes get you past an initial non-committal answer from someone who is not prepared for an interview.

THE IMPORTANCE OF RESEARCH

In whatever circumstances your interview is conducted, you should try to do some research on the person you will be talking to and the area in which he or she operates. For instance, if the interviewee is involved in a minority sport, you may have to learn its rules and something about the person's standing within the sport. Finding out as much about your subject as possible before going to the interview not only saves time, it also helps put the interviewee in the right frame of mind. Sports people who have their own websites, who are used to being interviewed on radio and television and seeing their names in the newspapers, often have an inflated view of how much the rest of the world knows about them. If your knowledge of their careers is less than they believe it ought to be, they will be less well disposed towards you, but if you pander to their egos by taking the trouble to find out about them in advance, the interview is likely to go more smoothly.

Research is particularly important if time is short. Doing as much background research on the subject as you can before you conduct the interview means that you don't have to waste time asking basic questions. And the more you appear to know about them and their sport, the less inhibited they are likely to be about covering areas which may be less familiar or even slightly embarrassing. You should, of course, check any facts you may be doubtful of, but when time is short the important thing is to get relevant and, if possible, lively quotes from your interviewee.

INTERVIEW TECHNIQUE

If you have never conducted an interview before, a useful place to start is by watching people interviewing and being interviewed on television, or by listening to interviews on radio. You should do this with a critical eye and ear, and try to work out what works and what does not. You can learn a lot from watching a skilled interviewer do his or her job, but don't just listen to the interviewer and slavishly imitate the types of question they ask and the way in which they ask them. You can often learn as much by listening to the answers, working out how people respond to questions phrased in different ways and the techniques they use to avoid giving a direct answer to a question.

You can also learn from a poor interviewer: not all radio and television journalists have perfect interviewing techniques. If an interviewee is giving one-word or one-sentence answers, or if they are avoiding giving a straight answer without difficulty, ask yourself how the questions could have been phrased to produce a more forthcoming response.

Bear in mind that, when conducting interviews, print journalists are often looking for something different from broadcast journalists. Someone interviewing on radio or television may be concerned principally with bringing out the personality of the interviewee, and the structure and length of a live interview may be as important as the answers. Neither of these things is particularly important to a print journalist, as the answers are unlikely to appear in his or her piece in the order in which they are given, and the majority of them will not be used. The print journalist may prefer to start by gathering background information, and then trying to tease out the short, telling quotes that will liven up the article.

All interviews are different. If you have set up a leisurely meeting in someone's home or office, you can afford to take your time and conduct the interview in the style of a normal conversation. This approach tends to relax people and encourages them to talk freely. But if you only have a couple of minutes on the phone or you are trying to interview someone on the hoof while they are leaving the training ground, you need to cut to the chase at once, and be much clearer about the basic information you are after. If you then find that the interviewee is compliant and willing to talk, you can supplement your basic questions later.

Some journalists have built their reputations on spiky interview techniques, but in general it doesn't pay to be too tough or antagonistic. You will get a better reception and a better response if you are friendly and put your interviewee at ease, although you should never come across as unprofessional or inefficient. If there are tough questions to be asked, save them until the end. If the interviewee clams up or walks out of the session when faced with a difficult question, you won't have lost much. If you ask the problematic questions at the beginning, you may come away with nothing.

If you take a mobile phone with you to an interview, turn it off before the interview begins. Being interrupted by calls is discourteous to the interviewee. They will also disrupt the flow of the interview. Getting back into the rhythm again may prove difficult.

QUESTIONS

It is a good idea to make a short list of key questions in advance, just to be sure you don't miss any vital information. But don't be too specific, as this may inhibit your interviewee from giving the sort of expansive answer that will often produce the best quotes. If you have plenty of time, it is often best to begin by asking for a general view on one of the topics you want to talk about: *Tell me in your own words what happened. How do you think the game went? What are your chances tomorrow? How's the training going?*

General questions like these allow the interviewee to open up and perhaps start talking about things that had not occurred to you, and which may open up new avenues for exploration. You can always move on to specifics later, and ask supplementary questions to fill in the gaps the interviewee has not covered. This approach also allows the interviewee to feel that he or she has some control over the direction the interview is taking.

Always ask open rather than CLOSED QUESTIONS. An OPEN QUESTION is one that cannot be answered by the words 'yes' or 'no'. Don't ask: *Was it the best moment of your life to win the Olympic gold medal?* Instead, ask: *How did it feel to win the Olympic gold?* This allows the subject to describe the feeling in their own words and is much more likely to produce an interesting quote.

Unless your interviewee is being exceptionally long-winded or straying too far from the subject, you should not interrupt while he or she is answering a question. The interviewee may have been about to say something interesting which an interruption will lose forever. It is better to take the opposite approach: allow the interviewee to finish, and then leave a little gap – a pregnant pause – before coming in with your next question. A conversational hiatus of this kind feels uncomfortable and will often encourage an interviewee to start talking again and perhaps volunteer something he or she would not otherwise have said.

Conversations are governed by informal conventions, of which a good interviewer needs to be aware. An interviewee will sometimes stop talking merely to be polite, to allow the interviewer back into the conversation. But in an interview – even a broadcast interview – the conversation should be as one-sided as possible. It is the interviewee's opinions we are interested in, not the journalist's.

Of course, interviewees will sometimes go off on their own hobby-horses. If an interview strays too far from where you want it to be, drag it back by asking a pointed question: *Can we get back to your injury problems?*

If interviewees are hostile because they don't like or trust journalists, or have had uncomfortable experiences with the media in the past, try to be reassuring. Don't risk antagonising your interviewee by defending the media too vigorously, and, above all, avoid the temptation to get involved in an argument.

NOTEBOOK OR RECORDER?

There is no point in setting up an interview unless you can make an accurate record of the replies to your questions. Until comparatively recently most journalists took short-hand notes. Now small, lightweight tape recorders, which can be placed unobtrusively on a table in front of the interviewee, are readily available and widely used. Most mobile phones will also record sound. As long as the device does not malfunction, recording an interview is easier and more thorough, and can be less unnerving to an interviewee than seeing someone scribbling spasmodically in a notebook.

But using a recorder has some disadvantages and is not always the best solution. If the interview lasts a while, listening to it again to select the quotes you wish to use can be time-consuming, especially if you are working to a tight deadline. It is often more efficient to develop the technique (using a recorder as back-up if you wish) of selective note-taking. This involves writing down the key answers from an interview so that they can be transcribed easily afterwards. It is sensible to take down more than you think you'll need, but try to get into the habit of editing out the material you are not going to need as the interview proceeds. It makes the material much easier and quicker to handle afterwards. If you have done your research in advance, and decided on the questions you need to ask, the most important role of the journalist in an interview is to *listen*.

USE YOUR EYES

But you should not only use your ears. You should also use your eyes. When you come to write your piece, you will want not only to report what your interviewee has said: you will want to paint a word picture of your subject as well. We can learn a lot from people's clothes and surroundings and general attitude. Make a note of the sort of clothes interviewees are wearing, what their house is like, what sort of car they drive, what sort of pictures they have on the walls, whether their trophies and medals are on display. Details like this enable readers to deduce whether they are proud or modest, whether they live entirely for their sport or whether they have other interests.

That is why television interviews often take place in someone's sitting room or workplace. What we see at the back of the shot conveys a lot of information about the person being interviewed. In print, describing the subject's surroundings helps to set the scene and allows readers to make their own judgements about the person's lifestyle.

TELEPHONE INTERVIEWS

Interviewing someone over the telephone is quick, and therefore useful if you are working to a tight deadline. It will sometimes be the only way you can get an interview but it is rarely as satisfactory as talking to someone face to face. The telephone doesn't encourage long conversational exchanges, and because you can't see the interviewee, you are deprived of one of your senses: the opportunity to paint a word picture of your subject is lost.

Unless your phone has a recording facility, you will have to make written notes of the interview. This can be difficult, and because accuracy is important, you should not be afraid to ask interviewees to repeat themselves or slow down while they are talking. If you are right-handed, hold the phone in your left hand so you can take notes, and use something to stop your notebook sliding around the desk.

WRITTEN QUESTIONS

Submitting written questions is the least satisfactory way of getting an interview, but it may be the only option open to you. Written answers tend to be flat and artificial, and – especially if the subject matter of the interview is controversial or delicate – may have been written by the subject's lawyer or public relations person. Supplementary questions are also difficult.

But potential interviewees who might otherwise be difficult to get hold of can often be reached via e-mail or their Twitter or Facebook accounts. The latter are easy enough to find, and if you have (or can guess) someone's e-mail address you can often by-pass their 'minders' and reach them direct. And because these are faster and less formal than most other forms of written communication, it is sometimes possible to get informal responses almost immediately. Sending supplementary questions is quick and easy too.

ENDING INTERVIEWS

Always end an interview of whatever sort by thanking interviewees for their time. It is polite, and you may want to interview them again. If it was a face-to-face interview, ask for a phone number in case there is anything you have forgotten and need to check later.

Many journalists like to keep chatting after the formal interview session has ended, while they are finishing their coffee or as they are being shown out of the building. This is because the interviewee will often loosen up after the notebook or recorder has been put away, and mention something of interest that did not come out in the interview. But if you intend to use anything you hear outside the formal interview situation it is courteous to tell the interviewee this, and respect any objection he or she makes.

WRITING IT UP

Try to transcribe the notes you made during the interview as soon as possible, while it is still fresh in your mind. Leave it a day or two and you may find them difficult to interpret, or you may forget the context in which something was said.

The act of transcription will also help you to order your thoughts and work out a structure, and maybe an INTRO, for your piece (which is another reason for using a notebook rather than, or as well as, a tape recorder). The same applies with broadcast interviews, where selecting the clips (see Chapter 9) you are going to use will help to determine the way in which you decide to write the script and tell the story.

Quotes help to give the flavour of the personality being interviewed, and your choice of quotes will have a major bearing on the impact of the piece. DIRECT QUOTATIONS – hearing the person's own words – make the biggest impact.

Colourful language and strong opinions should be quoted directly, rather than given as REPORTED SPEECH. Direct quotes provide immediacy and authenticity, but resist the temptation of quoting at too great a length, as this in itself can become boring. The best quotes are short, sharp and to the point.

Direct quotation means enclosing the actual words which were used between quotation marks, like this: 'Winning my first Wimbledon was the greatest moment of my life,' said the new champion. 'I just wanted to cry and kiss that famous turf.' The player's actual words are contained within quotation marks, as is the punctuation that belongs to them. Notice how the quote becomes weaker and less immediate if it is merely summarised in reported speech: The new champion said winning his first Wimbledon was the greatest moment of his life, making him want to cry and kiss the turf.

However, reported speech can be useful for condensing what someone says, or making sense of something that was not expressed particularly clearly by the interviewee.

Example

Question: 'How did you feel about your tackle that broke Tom Jones' leg?'

Answer: 'Yeah, it was bad. But that's the way it goes sometimes in this game. The ball was there. I went for it. There was no intent.'

Reported speech: Smith admitted the tackle was bad, but claimed he went for the ball and did not intend to break Jones' leg.

The answer is long-winded and not very elegantly phrased, but it can be summarised by the journalist like this, as on the left.

It is important when using reported speech not to distort the meaning of what the speaker said.

Sometimes it is useful to move between direct and reported speech by inserting a short, telling, direct quote into a piece of reported speech.

Example

The coach said 'awful decisions' by the referee had cost his team the match.

Remember that *direct speech* is always contained within quotation marks and written in the *present* tense. *Indirect speech* does not have quotation marks, and is written in the *past tense*.

Examples

'I *am* going to complain about some of the umpire's decisions,' said the coach.

The coach said he was going to complain about some of the umpire's decisions.

'I *will* be going for the world record in the hundred metres on Saturday,' she said.

She said she *would* be going for the world record in the hundred metres on Saturday.

Pronouns also change when reported speech is used. In the following example, *we* becomes *they*.

Example

'We have had the tightest defence in the league all season,' said the manager.

The manager said they had had the tightest defence in the league all season.

Moving between direct and indirect speech helps to vary the pace of an article and maintain the reader's interest. Continuous indirect speech can become boring, while continuous direct quotes often read like a verbatim report of the conversation and give the impression that the journalist has abdicated responsibility for selecting the best quotes and shaping the piece.

When attributing quotes, the word 'said' is usually adequate. It is simple and neutral. Any other word tends to seem intrusive unless there is a good reason for using it. If you are quoting extensively, it may be necessary to use alternatives such as 'commented', 'explained' or 'added' for variation. Beware of using 'loaded' attributions such as 'claimed' or 'alleged' unless there is some controversy about the facts being expressed, as these cast doubt on the validity of what the speaker is saying. Similarly, avoid words like 'admitted' or 'revealed' unless a genuine admission or revelation is involved.

QUOTING FAIRLY AND ACCURATELY

As a general rule, journalists should not tamper with the quotes they have collected in an interview. In particular, they should avoid trying to spice them up by putting words into people's mouths which they did not use. However, few people speak in grammatical sentences all the time, and we all add unnecessary words to buy ourselves thinking time. In such cases it is acceptable to tidy up the grammar and cut out the padding as long as the sense of the sentence is maintained.

Sometimes it is necessary for the journalist to edit what someone has said. If an interviewee makes a remark that could be defamatory, the journalist has a duty to cut it out. And sometimes people inadvertently say the opposite of what they mean, perhaps by adding or missing out the word 'not'. It is then imperative to correct them.

EXERCISE

Interview a friend or colleague about their favourite sports team. Make sure you have a sound background knowledge of the team's history and recent performances. Write out a short list of open-ended questions, designed to bring out firm and possibly controversial views, such as: 'Who are the strongest and weakest links in the defence?' or 'What else could the coach do to improve results?'

During the interview, try to take notes selectively, picking out the most powerful quotes and the most useful pieces of background information. Transcribe your notes as soon as possible after the interview, deciding which answers are strong enough to be used as direct quotes and which can be translated into reported speech. Make sure you use the correct tenses – the present tense for direct quotes, the past tense for reported speech. Decide whether any of the quotes suggest an intro for the piece. Ask the interviewee whether your transcription is a fair reflection of the interview, and if not, why not.

Summary

The interview is among the most important tools at the sports journalist's disposal. Knowing how to set up an interview, to put your subject at ease, to ask the right questions in the right way and to record the answers efficiently is vital if you are to get the most from face-to-face meetings with people whose time is often scarce. If it is not possible to arrange a meeting, there are other ways of getting the information you need for your piece. But however you obtain your information, it is important that you use it with integrity, and quote your subjects fairly and accurately.

6

Reporting the action

Chapter Summary

- The purpose of sports reporting
- Build-up or scene-setting pieces
- Previews
- 'Running' reports
- Considered reports
- Delayed reports
- Inquest pieces
- Favouritism and neutrality

Learning Objectives

- To recognise the function of sports reports
- To understand the media 'lifespan' of sporting events
- To identify the various forms of event reporting
- To understand why and how running copy is produced
- To identify the various forms of pre-event and post-event journalism
- To recognise the partiality of some sports reporting

Describing sporting events is one of the key skills of the sports writer, and provides the basic content of sports pages. Reports of events occupy more space in newspapers, radio and television than any other form of sports journalism. The ability to cover the action in a lively, informative and accurate way is an essential tool for any sports journalist.

The competitions which take place between individual athletes or teams is what sport is all about, and they are the springs from which all forms of sports journalism ultimately flow.

Often, the media will simply report the action on the day, but the more important events can command space on the sports pages for a much longer period. Indeed, major events such as the Olympic Games, the soccer, rugby and cricket World Cups, the baseball

World Series or the Superbowl in American football will occupy sports journalists for weeks or even months in advance of them taking place.

In such cases, the event itself forms only part of a continuum which, for the media, begins well before the action starts and continues after it has finished. It can consist of a number of different types of sports writing:

- Build-up or scene-setting pieces
- Previews
- 'Running' reports
- Considered reports
- Delayed reports
- Inquest pieces

THE BUILD-UP PIECE OR SCENE-SETTER

The media build-up to an event can consist of one or more pieces, often of FEATURE length, designed to generate interest in the event and provide readers with the background information they need to understand and enjoy it more fully. In setting the scene for these events, journalists will look for PEGS on which to hang their pieces, often focusing on an individual competitor as a means of injecting human interest. They may choose to write PROFILES of competitors who have a good chance of winning medals for the country in which the publication is based, or who have been enjoying a run of good form, or who did well the last time the event was staged, or who have recovered from a career-threatening injury or been in the news for reasons not directly related to sport, such as bad behaviour off the field. In the build-up to the Olympic Games or World Athletics Championships, the subject areas will range widely from the blue ribband track and field events to minor sports like pistol shooting or archery, which rarely warrant space on the sports pages.

Where team games are involved, the peg will often be a player or coach who has recently joined one of the teams, or who previously played for the opposition and who will therefore be able to offer insights into both camps. And because sport is often treated as soap opera by the media, scene-setters will sometimes concentrate on the 'back story' to the forthcoming episode – the highlights of previous encounters, or the grudges between teams or individuals.

Build-up pieces of this kind also satisfy the fans' thirst for knowledge about sports stars and fill space on the sports pages on slack days when there is little sporting action to report. The writing of profile or background pieces of this kind is covered in depth in Chapter 8.

EXERCISE

Choose a forthcoming major sporting event and compile a list of people-based articles which could be used to set the scene. Select your subjects from present and former competitors, managers and coaches. Then compare your list with the pieces run by newspapers, radio and television as the event approaches.

THE PREVIEW

Preview pieces focus more closely on the event itself and usually appear immediately before the event takes place. They cover topical issues such as the form and league positions of the teams involved, recent results, sequences of victories or defeats, team selection problems faced by coaches, such as injuries or suspensions to key players and transfers in or out of the club, and possible tactics and team formations. They also refer to players making their debuts, players who have played for both clubs, leading scorers, disciplinary records, the backgrounds of the officials who will be in charge, and whether the job of either coach is under threat. Sports writers rely for their information on their own expert knowledge and on the various sources outlined in Chapter 4. Preview pieces serve the same function, in an abbreviated form, as the official programmes offered for sale at sports events.

Example

Chelsea v Newcastle United
Kick off: 5.30 pm today
Referee: P. Dowd
TV: Live, ESPN Radio: talkSPORT

Chelsea manager Roberto Di Matteo will be looking to build on an impressive start to the Premier League season, and will play Spaniard Fernando Torres as a lone striker in front of close-season signing Eden Hazard. David Luiz is fit again and Chelsea look to record three straight league wins for the first time in 10 months.

Injuries and suspensions: Marko Marin injured and John Terry has a neck problem.

Probable team: (4-2-3-1): P Cech; B Ivanovic, G Cahill, D Luiz, A Cole; J O Mikel, F Lampard; Ramires, E Hazard, J Mata; F Torres

Top scorers: Torres, Lampard, Ivanovic 1

Newcastle boss Alan Pardew has Demba Ba and Fabricio Coloccini back from injury, but is unhappy that policing commitments for the Notting Hill Carnival mean this match takes place just two days after his side's Europa League trip to Athens.

Injuries and suspensions: Cheick Tiote and Shola Ameobi both doubtful.

Probable team (4-4-2): T Krul; D Simpson, S Taylor, F Coloccini, D Santon; H Ben Arfa, C Tiote, Y Cabaye, J Gutierrez; D Ba, P Cisse

Top scorers: Ba, Ben Arfa 1

Forecast: Chelsea to continue their flying start

As we shall see, previews are useful not only for the readers who may be attending the event or watching on television; they are also invaluable for the journalists who will be reporting on it.

WHY REPORT SPORT?

The hub round which this sequence of pieces revolves is the event itself. Before we consider *how* sporting events are reported, it is worth asking *why* they are reported, because that should determine how the job is done.

What is a report of a match or a race supposed to do? If we already know the result, why should we be interested in how it was achieved? There are several reasons.

First, a report offers a *vicarious experience* for readers who were not able to attend or watch the event themselves. Reports should therefore offer vivid descriptions of the key moments of the event.

It also gives those who were able to attend or who watched the event on television an opportunity to *relive* the experience, and to compare their impressions with those of an expert observer. Reports are often read most keenly by those who were there. If we have been to a football game, the report of that game is the first we turn to in the following day's newspapers. People who live in towns which still have Saturday evening sports papers, often printed on coloured paper and with names like the *Sporting Pink* or *Green' Un*, which provide running reports (see below) of matches, will often buy a copy on the way home from the stadium. They do so to read a move-by-move account of the game they have just watched and relive it over again, perhaps picking up additional information they missed earlier. Reports must be accurate and well-informed if they are to impress the reader who has witnessed the event.

Some readers want to test the *opinions* they formed while watching the event against those of an expert. Reports can generate debate and provide a printed equivalent of the post-match discussion in the pub. People also read reports for *information* – that an athlete recorded a personal best, that a batsman has scored his thousandth run of the season, that a team has won promotion to a higher league. Many people read reports for *entertainment*, even though they may not be especially interested in the outcome of the event. They read them for the quality of the writing, for the wit or humour or wisdom of a talented writer who happens to be a sports journalist. Reports should also offer *analysis* and *criticism* of tactics and performances, and put the outcome of the event into *context* – what does it mean for a team's prospects for promotion or relegation, or an athlete's chances of qualifying to take part in the Olympic Games?

REPORTING THE EVENT

Covering a sporting event for a daily newspaper is one of the most demanding and pressurised jobs sports writers have to do. It involves writing a predetermined number of words quickly and accurately while the action on which they are reporting is still unfolding before their eyes. It demands not only a comprehensive knowledge of the sport being covered, its rules and history, and a similar knowledge of the individuals taking part, but also the ability to write accurately and entertainingly against tight deadlines and to a specific length. The production demands of newspapers may also require reporters to write two or more different versions of their reports within a very short space of time.

Production demands

Because professional sport is a branch of the entertainment and leisure industry, most sporting events take place at the most convenient times for the public to watch – weekends and midweek evenings. This places difficult demands on daily and Sunday newspapers wishing to cover the events. Their first editions may go to press less than an hour after games and meetings end.

To enable them to carry reports of these events in their early editions, sports desks must take in and process the copy produced by their reporters quickly and efficiently. This depends to a large degree on forward planning by the production staff on sports desks in newspaper offices and fast work by reporters in the field.

Once the events to be covered have been chosen, sports pages are planned in advance, with a specific amount of space allocated to each match. This means that reporters at the stadiums can be told the precise number of words they must file on their event. And to maximise the time SUB-EDITORS on sports desks have to process the large volumes of copy flowing in on a busy afternoon or evening of sport, reporters are expected to file their first reports as running copy.

Running copy

Running copy (often referred to by journalists as 'a runner') involves filing copy in a series of TAKES, originally by telephone to a COPYTAKER, but now more likely from a laptop straight into the newspaper's computer system. A journalist will contact the office from the press box before the event begins to be told how many words to write.

It is important that the correct number of words is filed. If not, a sub-editor will have to cut or add to the copy to make it fit the space available, wasting valuable production time. Reporters filing copy electronically can get an accurate word count from their laptop computers. Those dictating copy straight from their notes will ask the copytaker to give them a word count from the computer into which the copy is being keyed. Those writing copy by hand before dictating it can calculate the length quickly by writing it at five words per line in their notebooks.

If a reporter is asked to write a 550-word 'runner' on a soccer match, for instance, he or she will be expected to file the first take of 250 words at half time, the second take of 250 words ten minutes from the end, and a final take of 50 words, together with the scoreline, the moment the referee blows the whistle at the end of the game.

An even more extreme example of this is the report written for the Saturday afternoon sports papers produced in some large cities, which are printed within minutes of games ending so that they can be sold to fans as they go home from matches. The reporters involved are in constant telephone contact with their offices, and report the game incident by incident as it happens. (This process has now been adopted by websites, which produce minute-by-minute reports which can be read on a variety of mobile devices – see Chapter 10.)

In such cases, journalists are essentially reporting the key moments of the match in chronological order, as they unfold before them on the pitch, without knowing what the final result will be. The final 50 words will sum up the game and serve as the INTRO (introduction) to the piece. It will be placed at the top of the copy by the sub-editor who handles it.

Example

Running copy – 550 words

First take – 300 words at half time

Chelsea, who hadn't won three league matches in a row for nearly a year, started as though they were determined to rectify that and show that winning the European Champions League was no fluke. Branislav Ivanovic forced a save from Newcastle keeper Tim Krul in less than three minutes, and summer signing Eden Hazard had a free kick blocked by Steven Taylor before bringing another save out of Krul.

So it was no surprise when the Belgian opened Chelsea's account after 21 minutes, calmly sliding home the penalty awarded after Fernando Torres was brought down by Vurnon Anita.

Newcastle, having to play one of their toughest games of the season just two days after travelling to Athens for a Europa League fixture, scarcely troubled the Chelsea defence, and Demba Ba, back in the side after injury, was wide of the target with the couple of chances that came his way. Papiss Cisse's radar was functioning rather better, and he had a shot blocked by Gary Cahill and another saved by Petr Cech.

But with Chelsea making most of the early running, it was Torres, winner of the Golden Boot at this summer's European Championships, who seemed most anxious to get on the scoresheet – maybe a little too anxious, as the referee instead entered his name in his book for what was adjudged to be a dive. After waltzing round Fabricio Coloccini, the striker belatedly went to ground after the slightest of contacts.

But the Spaniard made amends two minutes into first-half stoppage time with a goal well worthy of an award. After a series of one-touch passes down the right, Hazard's neat back-heel fell to Torres, who curled the ball from the outside of his right boot into the top right corner, giving Krul no chance.

Second take – 200 words, ten minutes from the end

Newcastle shook off their jet-lag after the break, led by their most creative player, Hatem Ben Arfa, who wriggled into the Chelsea box, only to drag his shot wide of Petr Cech's upright. But the goalkeeper was forced into action after slack Chelsea defending allowed Ba to break clear and squeeze in a shot from a tight angle. Cech flung himself to his right and blocked the ball with his body at the near post.

But Chelsea remained dangerous on the counter-attack. More slick work from Torres allowed Ashley Cole to shoot across the face of goal, and Hazard showed electric pace to streak past Coloccini to the byline. He cut the ball back, but Gutierrez was able to scramble the ball away.

Newcastle survived again when Ryan Bertrand was released down the left and his shot from the angle of the penalty area was palmed away athletically by Krul.

The visitors should have pulled one back when Ba found himself unmarked on the penalty spot after several Chelsea defenders again failed to clear, but his first touch was poor and he could only scuff what was perhaps his side's best opportunity into the waiting arms of Cech.

Intro – 50 words at the final whistle

Chelsea opened up a three-point lead at the top of the Premiership thanks to first-half goals from strikers Eden Hazard and Fernando Torres. They maintained their 100 per cent start to the season with an impressive display which will take them into Friday's European Super Cup showdown with Atletico Madrid with confidence.

Discussion

The time constraints imposed on journalists writing running copy mean that they sometimes have to write much of it before anything of real significance has happened. In this example, however, there was plenty of action from the start, although the reporter leads into it with background material about Chelsea's relatively poor Premier League campaign the previous season – material which would have been gathered for the preview piece discussed earlier. This is followed by a description of key moments in the first half of the match, to make up the number of words required at half time. It is usual to use a player's full name when first mentioned, but only his surname afterwards. Notice how the reporter has linked the early action involving Hazard to the opening goal with the sentence: *So it was no surprise when the Belgian opened Chelsea's account....*

Providing bridging passages like this avoids the jerkiness that would otherwise result from an abrupt change of direction in the piece. Although the overall word count is fixed, reporters are permitted a certain amount of flexibility in the length of their separate takes. In this example, there was plenty of first-half action, so the reporter was able to produce 300 words without too much padding out the action with background material. If even more goals had been scored, and there had been a number of other notable incidents, the reporter may have chosen to file as many as 350 words at half time. But the second take would have been reduced in length accordingly, to avoid exceeding the overall word count for the piece.

The challenges facing sports reporters vary according to the way the events they are watching unfold, and sport by nature is unpredictable. A dearth of goals or any other exciting incidents means the challenge is one of producing an interesting and readable piece out of scant raw material. This may mean a heavier reliance on analysis of the teams' tactics or the performance of individual players. At many sporting events, however, the challenge is to condense a great deal of action and incident into a relatively small number of words.

The final take of a running match report will often demand the ability to condense the entire event into a couple of sentences, as well as putting the result into perspective. This final take will appear in the newspaper as the introduction to the report, and it is the function of an intro to distil the essence of the story while grabbing the attention of readers and making them want to read on. In this example, the writer has encapsulated the essence of the match and its effect on the league table in the first sentence, and used the second sentence to speculate on the game's significance for a European Super Cup match in a few days' time.

Finally, it is worth remembering that journalists are expected to stick to the number of words for which they have been asked, no matter how many or how few goals have been scored, and no matter how exciting or dull the match.

EXERCISE

Watch a game on television, either live or recorded. Before you do so, study preview pieces in newspapers, on teletext or on the internet, making notes of any background information which may be useful in a running report. This should include the names of the players on both teams and their shirt numbers, so that you can identify them easily. Set yourself an overall length for your piece of 500 words and write a report on the game as you watch, in takes of 250 words (to be completed by the end of half time), 200 words completed 10 minutes before the final whistle and a 50-word intro, completed as soon as the game ends.

You will find it more realistic, and less distracting, if you turn off the commentary. You will still have the advantage, not always available to reporters in a press box, of action replays of the key moments. But you will not, of course, have access to the shared expert knowledge available among the pool of journalists covering the match at the stadium.

Take care to hit the deadlines and 'take' lengths you have been set. Compare your finished piece with reports of the match in the following day's newspapers.

THE REPORTER'S NOTEBOOK

While games are in progress, reporters should make notes of the key incidents, together with the times at which they happened, in their notebooks. Some reporters dictate running copy straight from their notes, though most write out their takes before dictating them or filing them electronically.

It is vital to take accurate notes of the action, as journalists will almost certainly have to refer back to them at later stages of the reporting process. The first thing most reporters do is make a note of the team formations, using the players' shirt numbers as shorthand. Players' names are also written in shorthand form, so that the reporter misses as little of the action as possible while jotting down the key incidents. Journalists organise their notebooks in different ways, but a typical page of notes from the match covered above would look like this:

Example

Chelsea	Newcastle
1	1
3-4-24-2	3-2-27-5
34-12-16	18-8-4-10
17-9-10	19-9
(4-3-3)	(4-4-2)
Shot from long distance by Meireles misses to the right (4 mins)	Ba shoots over bar (12)
Hazard shot, Taylor block (5)	Ba shot blocked by Cahill (19)
Hazard shot, Krul save (14)	Cisse shot, Cahill blocks (40)
Torres rounds Anita, tripped, penalty. Hazard scores to keeper's right (22)	Cisse shot, Cech save (43)
Cole – Ivanovic – Krul saves (30)	Arfa wide of post (51)
Torres booked for diving (39)	Simpson cross, Cisse header, misses left (54)
Passing move down right, Hazard backheel, Torres scores outside of right foot into top corner (45+2)	Ba shot, Cech save, corner (59)
Half time 2-0	Sub: Taylor for Simpson (63)
Sub: Ramires for Mata (66)	Sub: Marveaux for Santon (74)
Bertrand cuts in, shoots, Krul diving save (80)	Sub: Perch for Cabaye (76)
Sub: Lampard for Meireles (87)	Ba shot, Cech save (84)
Full time 2-0	Arfa cross, Cahill clearance (90+3)

When reporting matches, many reporters divide their notebooks into two columns, one for each team. This makes it easier to locate notes of specific incidents when writing their reports.

The figures at the top of each column are the shirt numbers of the players and the positions they occupy on the field. Most newspapers carry this information at the end of match reports, and a visual record of the team formations helps reporters identify players during a match.

Reporters make brief notes of key moments in a match, together with the time at which they happened. They will often shorten the names of players or their positions (gk = goalkeeper). This cuts note-taking to a minimum and allows them to concentrate on the action and writing their reports.

CONSIDERED REPORTS

The constraints under which running copy has to be written can sometimes produce unbalanced accounts of the event, with formulaic intros and abrupt conclusions. Given time to consider the match as a whole, journalists can produce better-balanced, more reflective and more thoughtfully written accounts. They can also include the post-match views of the coaches and players on the performances of their teams. The time available between the first and final editions of their papers (although this may be as little as an hour) gives them the chance to do this. During that time they have to rewrite their pieces and carry out their interviews.

Fortunately, the administrators of professional sports are aware of these time constraints and do what they can to accommodate the post-match needs of journalists. Most sports organisations require managers and coaches, and in some cases players, to make themselves available for media interview within a reasonable period after game's end. Major stadiums have press rooms or media centres in which journalists can work, and many have specially equipped interview theatres to which coaches and players will be brought after a game. In smaller stadiums, however, post-match interviews can take place in the manager's office, the players' tunnel or even on the pitch. In America, journalists often have open access to the dressing rooms, where they can talk to anyone they wish.

The purpose of post-match interviews is to give journalists the opportunity of questioning the key figures about major incidents and report their views on the significance of the result and the performances of individuals. It also allows them to gather information and responses on any injuries sustained or disciplinary action taken by match officials, and to seek comment about controversial aspects of the game. The appropriate quotes can then be included in a considered rewrite of their earlier running reports.

If time is available, many journalists will produce a completely fresh report for the later edition, interweaving quotes with a more balanced account of the most significant moments in the game and some comment and analysis of their own. Others may choose to retain some of their earlier material, cutting and condensing it to focus on the most significant aspects of the match and making space for quotes, analysis and action from the latter part of the game that they did not previously have time or space to report. They will often spend much of their time polishing the opening of their reports, to make them more balanced, to take in significant post-match quotes and to sharpen the impact on their readers and make them want to read on. Reporters who work for newspapers which produce regional editions may have to provide two versions of their considered reports, written from the point of view of each of the teams involved.

These considered pieces are usually expected to be of the same length as the earlier running copy, although sports editors will sometimes give reporters at particularly eventful games more space for their rewrites, while those at less eventful ones may have the space available to them reduced.

Here is the considered rewrite of the game for which we have already seen the running copy.

Example

Chelsea 2 Newcastle United 0

On this showing, the rest of England's top clubs should be afraid – very afraid. There's a new danger man in the Premier League. His name is Eden Hazard, and the warning lights are flashing.

The 21-year-old Belgian midfielder scored one goal and created the other to help Chelsea to their third straight win of the fledgling season, something they last achieved 10 months ago.

When Fernando Torres was brought down in the box by Vurnon Anita's ill-judged tackle after 22 minutes it was Hazard, who has now scored all 11 of his penalties in league football, who calmly converted the kick.

Two minutes into first-half added time he returned the compliment, back-heeling cleverly into the path of Torres, who struck the sweetest of shots with the outside of his right boot into the top corner of the net.

It was no more than Chelsea manager Roberto Di Matteo expected: 'He hasn't surprised us. We watched him a lot last season and it's a different league, so you're not quite sure how he'll adapt to the Premier League, but he seems to have found his feet very quickly. He's a wonderful player for us,' he said.

Hazard is already well on the way to repaying the £32 million Chelsea paid Lille for him in the close season. As a playmaker, he has been involved in most of the goals Chelsea have scored this season, and now he's on the scoresheet himself.

Many feared Chelsea would struggle for goals after the departure of Didier Drogba, but Hazard looks a more-than-adequate replacement. He has deftness of touch, sublime control and electric pace, as he showed when he streaked past Fabricio Coloccini in the second half to cut the ball back from the byline and cause more panic in the Newcastle defence before Jonas Gutierrez scrambled it away.

Newcastle manager Alan Pardew summed it up. 'There is a nonchalance about Hazard that marks him down as a great player. He will make a difference to Chelsea compared to last season.'

(Continued)

(Continued)

Newcastle's pedigree is more difficult to assess. Understandably, they looked jet-lagged in the first half just two days after travelling to Athens for a Europa League fixture, and Pardew was less than pleased that policing demands of this weekend's Notting Hill Carnival meant the match had to be played yesterday.

Demba Ba, back in the side after injury, and Papiss Cisse both squandered chances, but their most creative player was Hatem Ben Arfa, who wriggled into the Chelsea box, only to drag his shot wide of Petr Cech's upright.

The visitors looked brighter in the second half and should have pulled one back when Ba found himself unmarked on the penalty spot, but his first touch was poor and he could only scuff what was perhaps his side's best opportunity into the waiting arms of Cech. It was the story of Ba's, and Newcastle's, afternoon.

The only cloud on Chelsea's horizon was the yellow card shown to Torres, who was booked for a dive when trying to get round Fabricio Coloccini. The striker belatedly went to ground after the slightest of contacts.

This morning, Chelsea stand three points clear at the top of the Premiership table, though they've played one game more than their rivals. With Hazard in their side and in this form, Chelsea are a clear and present danger.

EXERCISE

Try to identify the main differences between the running copy and the rewrite.

Suggested answer

1 The reporter has reworded the opening paragraph, to make it brighter and more interesting, and to focus the report around the performance of one of the key players. The intro becomes an extended pun on Hazard's name – *the warning lights are flashing* – coupled to a quote from a well-known movie – *be afraid, very afraid* – to grab the reader's attention.

2 The second paragraph briefly summarises the key points – again from Hazard's perspective – and sets the result in context. This leads naturally into the third and fourth paragraphs, which describe the two goals.

3 The reporter has now had time to attend the post-match press conferences, so a managerial quote can now be included to support the reporter's own verdict and provide information the reader may not already be aware of from other sources.

4 The action has been repackaged. Instead of the chronological account of the ebb and flow of play, the reporter now concentrates on an analysis of the performance of the key player, and fleshes this out with more background about him. This is followed

by a quote from the Newcastle manager about Hazard, which allows for a smooth transition to an analysis of Newcastle with the phrase: *Newcastle's pedigree is more difficult to assess.*

5 Whereas the running copy was written rather blandly, the reporter has had time to polish up the prose of the considered piece with a bit of alliteration (*calmly converting the kick*) in paragraph 3. The running copy ended rather abruptly on a wasted chance but the considered piece is rounded off neatly by finishing, as the report started, with another movie metaphor – *a clear and present danger*.

DELAYED REPORTS

Considered pieces like this usually appear in the following day's newspapers. They are the first written accounts most readers will have seen of the event, and they will expect the action to be thoroughly covered. However, newspapers sometimes decide or are compelled to carry reports some time after the event has taken place. Daily newspapers which do not publish on Sundays often choose to carry reports of Saturday's matches on Mondays, and weekly newspapers are often compelled to carry reports several days after the event. The time difference between the place where an event is happening and the place where a newspaper is published will sometimes result in reports appearing up to 36 hours after the event. Accounts of the first day's play in a Test cricket match in Australia, for instance, will not appear in British newspapers until after the second day's play has been completed.

By the time these reports appear, the reader may well have seen highlights of the event on television or read reports in other newspapers, on teletext or the internet. Delayed reports, therefore, have to take a different approach and find ways of offering a fresh perspective on the event. There is still the need to provide basic information about the event, such as the result, the scorers and other key incidents, but the main aim should be to provide readers with fresh information the contemporaneous reports did not supply. This may involve deeper analysis, a more in-depth look at controversial or key incidents or the performances of individual players, the effects of injuries on the respective squads, a consideration of forthcoming matches in the light of what happened in the one being reported, or a piece devoted largely to the thoughts of the coaches or players after the game. Delayed reports should always try to move the story on.

Because they are aware of the needs of the media, many coaches and managers will give separate interviews, after the normal post-match press conference has finished, for journalists writing delayed reports and those who need to find fresh angles around which to base those reports.

The following is a delayed report of the soccer match described above. The game took place on a Saturday afternoon, but the report was written for the Monday morning edition of a British national broadsheet newspaper, and would be read almost two days after the event took place. Compare it with the considered report of the same match printed above, looking particularly at what proportion of the delayed report is devoted to incidents in the game itself, and how much is given over to quotes, analysis and discussion of points which arose as a result of the game.

Example

Chelsea 2 Newcastle United 0

After the wettest summer on record, the rain clouds were still hanging over Stamford Bridge on Saturday. But for Chelsea, and for their problematic Spanish striker Fernando Torres, the forecast is a lot brighter.

Chelsea sit on top of the Premier League with a 100 per cent record after three matches, and Torres is brimming with confidence again after scoring his second goal of the campaign.

And what a goal it was, curled into the top corner of Tim Krul's net off the outside of his right boot with the sort of flair that typified Chelsea's new approach to the game.

And, darting past Vurnon Anita in the box, he also won the penalty which allowed his new striking partner Eden Hazard to convert from the spot to begin this comfortable victory.

It is a far cry from the end of last season, when Torres was left out of the starting line-up for the Champions League final and Chelsea were packing men behind the ball and grinding out results as they struggled to their lowest Premier League finish for years.

How times have changed. The departure of Didier Drogba, who almost single-handedly won that Champions League final, seemed certain to compound Chelsea's problems, but the arrival of Hazard to replace him already seems like an inspired move on the part of manager Roberto Di Matteo.

Willing to run at defenders and shoot on sight, Hazard has taken Chelsea out of reverse gear and switched them into overdrive. They can still defend, as they did in the second half against a resurgent Newcastle, but flair is now an equal part of the package.

'The confidence is back because I am playing more, and with the new players we have signed we are more attacking,' said Torres.

His manager agreed. 'Players thrive on confidence, and for strikers it's important to score. At the moment, he's providing and scoring.'

It is still early days, of course, and their first two opponents – Wigan and Reading – were not the toughest they will face. Newcastle, who exceeded expectations last season, are made of sterner stuff and tested the Chelsea defence in the second half. Demba Ba had two good chances, but goalkeeper Petr Cech made two fine saves.

Forced to play just two days after their Europa League trip to Athens, they were not at their freshest, and manager Alan Pardew is realistic about what this season holds.

'We are in that group with Tottenham, Everton and Liverpool. It will be tough to reach the dizzy heights of Man City, Man United and Chelsea, but you've got to believe you can.'

For now, though, the belief is all with Torres and Chelsea.

Discussion

With the match having taken place nearly 48 hours previously, the reporter concentrates on analysis and looking forward to the prospects for both clubs for the rest of the fledgling season. In the intro, the reporter is implicitly forecasting what the new season holds in store for Chelsea by employing a metaphor about the weather, something all readers of the piece will be familiar with, to contrast the way Chelsea and Torres are playing compared with last season. The reporting of the match action is limited because, as we have seen, readers have had ample opportunity to see or read about this already.

The bulk of the remainder of the report is taken up with the views of the key player mentioned in the piece, and the respective managers. The quotes have been chosen to illustrate the points being made by reporter and player. The Newcastle manager's own forecast of his side's prospects leads neatly into the OUTRO, which brings the piece back full circle to the player mentioned in the intro.

 **E**X**ERCISE**

Using your own analytical skills, and quotes derived from the media or club websites, write a delayed report on the event for which you have already produced running copy and considered pieces, for publication 24 hours after the event.

INQUEST PIECES

Some sporting events, such as international matches or the finals of major competitions, acquire such significance that the media will take the process further by devoting space in the days following their initial reports to deeper analysis. This may focus on what the performance and result mean for the future of the team or athlete involved, or extend to wider issues such as the state of the sport nationally or worldwide.

Example

South Africa's thrilling win over England in the Third Test at Lord's meant they displaced their opponents at the top of the International Cricket Council's Test rankings. But how long can they stay there?

There is no doubt that the South Africans deserved their 2-0 series victory. They were the better team in both batting and bowling, their fielding was outstanding and they threw off their reputation for 'choking' at crucial moments.

But gone are the days when a single nation, like the West Indies or Australia, could dominate world cricket for a decade. It's tight at the top now, as the close finish to this series showed, and South Africa are the fourth side in the last three years to top the ICC rankings.

But the last time they did so – in 2009 – they didn't play a single Test as leaders before being overhauled by India. Can they last longer this time?

On paper, maybe. South Africa are a good all-round side, with Hashim Amla, captain Graeme Smith, Jacques Kallis and AB de Villiers all in the top 10 of world Test batsmen. In addition, Dale Steyn and Vernon Philander occupy the top two spots in the world bowling rankings, and Kallis is also one of the world's great all-rounders.

Coach Gary Kirsten, who also led India to great things, knows how to get the best out of them, but Smith and Kallis are both reaching the end of their careers, and we may have seen South Africa at their peak.

That will be tested when they go to Australia, who are well into their rebuilding process after dominating world cricket for so long, for a series in November. The Aussies are still some way short of the strength in depth they once had, but Michael Clarke remains one of the world's top batsmen, and Ben Hilfenhaus and Peter Siddle have long been instilling fear with the ball. Home advantage may prove crucial.

England go to India – the other contenders for the crown – this winter. In Jimmy Anderson and Stuart Broad they still have one of the world's best pace attacks, and Graeme Swann can spin the ball, but their top-order batsmen have not been delivering, and they must learn to hold their catches.

Kevin Pietersen, their best batsman, now has an uncertain future after dressing-room unrest, and Andrew Strauss may be considering his future as captain after this series defeat. But with an Ashes series coming up next year, they could yet regain top spot sooner rather than later.

But it is certain to remain a four-horse race. Pakistan are handicapped by corruption scandals and security considerations which means they must play all their matches away from home, while internal disputes mean the Windies are still shadows of their former selves.

Even so, the ICC mace may be covering a lot of air miles in the next two or three years. And that can only be good for the game.

Discussion

This piece uses the peg provided by South Africa's victory to examine the state of Test cricket around the world. It ranges back over the previous four years, and also looks forward to what the future may hold, particularly in the light of upcoming Test series. It moves way beyond the England v South Africa Test series, out of which it arose, to include the state of the world's other major cricketing nations.

FAVOURITISM OR NEUTRALITY

Although sports reporters are normally expected to behave like other journalists and produce even-handed and unbiased stories, there are occasions when they are permitted – and expected – to stray from absolute neutrality. The readers of local newspapers will largely support local teams or athletes, sometimes with great fervour, and they expect to have their prejudices reflected by the local media. If a team from within a newspaper's circulation area is playing one from elsewhere, the event would normally be reported from the perspective of the local team. Similarly, national newspapers will report events involving a 'home' team or participants from a national perspective. But when reporting domestic events in which they have no way of knowing which, if any, of the participants the reader supports, reporters should remain strictly neutral.

Summary

Reporting the action at sporting events is one of the key roles of sports journalists. It involves a wide range of activities, from previews and build-up pieces which set the scene for the event, to 'instant' reports of the action, more considered accounts, and reflective pieces written after the event. It demands the ability to write quickly and accurately, and within strict space limitations.

7

Sports news and photography

Chapter Summary

- Writing news stories
- Writing intros
- The five Ws
- What not to do
- News story structure
- Writing style
- Running stories and follow-ups
- Journalistic ethics
- The role of the sports photographer

Learning Objectives

- To learn the basic principles of news story writing
- To understand the importance of the intro
- To know how to structure a news story
- To recognise the stylistic demands of a news story
- To understand the nature of running stories and follow-ups
- To appreciate the role of the sports photographer

Reports of the action on track or field form the staple diet of the sports pages, but when there is little action to report, and when big stories are breaking outside the arena, other journalistic skills are called for. In addition to the specialist skills of a sports reporter, the sports journalist must also be able to handle the most fundamental of journalistic skills – researching and writing news stories.

The action off the field is almost as important as that on it, and there is always a steady flow of news stories awaiting the attention of the sports journalist. There is the movement of players from one club to another, the hiring and firing of coaches, the signing of sponsorship deals, the off-field behaviour (or misbehaviour) of players and fans, changes to the rules of sports, the financial difficulties in which clubs and governing bodies sometimes find themselves, drugs tests, and the daily activities of sports people who have become personalities and celebrities in their own right. Covering these stories demands the same nose for news and the same tenacity as that needed by any other reporter on a newspaper or broadcasting station.

WRITING NEWS STORIES

The news story is the basic building block of all journalism. News stories follow a simple structure, and anyone who can write a good news story can communicate clearly about anything. It is worth spending time learning how to do it well.

The secret of writing a good news story is knowing how to condense the essence of the story into the intro – a single sentence or short paragraph. Additional information can then be added, in order of importance. The essence of a good news story is that, at whatever point the reader chooses to abandon it, what he or she has read will make complete sense.

There are two reasons why news stories are written this way. The first is that it allows readers to take as much or as little as they wish from the story before they move on to the next one. The second is more practical: if space is tight, a sub-editor can cut the story at any point, from the bottom up, without having to rewrite it, knowing that it will be understood by the reader. For this reason, news reporters must learn to swallow their pride. Those who write sports news stories should *expect* to have their copy cut by sub-editors, and they should always be written so that they can be cut easily.

At first, many students find it difficult to write a simple news story. This is because the news story's structure is, in many ways, the opposite of how they have always been taught to write. A school or university essay often begins with a statement of what it intends to achieve, goes on to provide a series of facts in support of an argument, and ends by drawing a conclusion from them. The news story, on the other hand, *begins* with the conclusion – with a statement of the essential things the reader needs to know. It then goes on to provide additional information to justify and explain what we have already been told in the opening paragraph.

WRITING INTROS

The intro, or opening paragraph, is the key to a good news story. It should condense the story to its basic facts and make the reader want to know more. Achieving this is not as easy as it sounds, and for most people it only comes with practice.

The simplest way to grasp how an intro should be written is to imagine you are telling the story to a friend. When we have some interesting news, it is natural to blurt out the key points first: 'Did you hear that Andrew Strauss has resigned as England cricket captain and retired from all cricket? Alastair Cook is taking over.'

With only minor modifications, this would serve as the intro for the story in the following day's newspapers:

> Andrew Strauss yesterday resigned as England cricket captain and retired from all cricket. Alastair Cook will take over for the tour of India later this year.

Those two short sentences contain all we need to know to understand the essence of the story. Additional facts will put what has happened into perspective and explain the reasons behind it, but if we never read any further, we will understand the essential points.

The five Ws

A more systematic way of achieving the same thing is to answer the following questions, sometimes referred to as the five Ws.

Who?

What?

When?

Where?

Why?

Answering these questions – and the supplementary question How? – usually allows us to assemble all the information needed to understand a story, although it is not always necessary to answer all of them in the intro. The example above answers the first three questions in the brief opening sentence. Andrew Strauss (*who*) yesterday (*when*) resigned as England captain (*what*). The second sentence answers the same questions about his replacement. Alastair Cook (*who*) will take over (*what*) for the tour of India later this year (*when*).

Having written the intro, the essence of the story can then be amplified in the second paragraph, which in this case might read:

> Strauss announced his decision at a press conference at Lord's. 'I haven't batted well enough for a long time now. I think I have run my race,' he said.

This paragraph answers the other three questions not dealt with in the intro. Strauss announced his decision at a press conference (*how*) at Lord's (*where*) because he was not batting well enough (*why*). If a story is just breaking, the *why* aspect may have to be missed out because it involves analysis or demands information that is not immediately available to the reporter. Follow-up stories (see below) will often concentrate on *why* something happened.

Intros should always start with the main point: in this case, *Andrew Strauss resigned*. Do not attempt to lead up to the main point with explanation. Something like *After England lost their place as Number 1 in the world rankings, their captain Andrew Strauss submitted his resignation* merely delays the impact of the story and makes the intro unfocused. All explanation and description should be saved until after the reader has absorbed the main impact of the story.

In most sports news stories this will mean that the intro will focus on people: the quarterback who has been traded, the coach who has been sacked, the jockey who has been suspended, the athlete who has failed a drugs test.

What not to do

Avoid starting intros with questions or quotes. Readers want to be told what has happened, not cross-examined. Quotes in a news story slow down the process of absorbing the main facts.

Care should also be taken about saying *when* a story took place. To use the word 'yesterday' in a morning newspaper is acceptable because readers know that they are reading yesterday's news. But few evening newspapers would use the word – even though many of their stories happened the previous day – because it draws attention to the fact that the story is 24 hours old and robs it of the immediacy that news stories strive for. Similarly, a weekly newspaper published on a Friday would try to avoid saying that the story had happened on Monday. One way round this, and of restoring immediacy to a story, is to find a way of getting the word *today* into the intro:

> England opener Alastair Cook is today coming to terms with his new responsibilities as captain after Andrew Strauss dramatically quit the job at the end of the series against South Africa.

NEWS STORY STRUCTURE

Having summarised the main points of the story in the intro, the reader should then be provided with the detail in order of its importance. In this case, Andrew Strauss is the key figure, and his resignation and the reasons for it should now be amplified.

Example

The 35-year-old Middlesex batsman has ended his three-and-a-half-year reign as England's Test captain, and retired from all forms of cricket.

He said: 'It hasn't been something that occurred overnight. It has built over a few months. I would like to go out on my own terms with my head held high and I think this is the right time.'

The second most important figure is the man who will replace him as captain, Alastair Cook. We now need to hear his reaction and, for the benefit of readers with a limited knowledge of cricket, learn something about him.

> ## Example
>
> The England captaincy will be taken over by 27-year-old Alastair Cook, who has already captained the England one-day and Twenty20 sides, and led the Test team on a tour of Bangladesh.
>
> He said: 'It is a great honour to be appointed Test captain and I am very much looking forward to captaining the side in India this winter and beyond.'

If space is limited, the story could end here, but because the success of their national sports teams is important to readers, a British newspaper would want to run the story at length. The scope of the piece would therefore be widened to include the reactions of other key figures in English cricket. Social media sites can be very useful here, as sports professionals are often quick to comment via Twitter or other sites on breaking news stories, especially if they are affected themselves. The records of the two key figures would have to be explained, together with any background information which may put the story into context (see the reference to the Kevin Pietersen controversy below). Journalists might also seek the views of respected analysts on Strauss's captaincy and the prospects for the team when Cook takes over.

The remainder of the story might run something like this:

> ## Example
>
> England fast bowler James Anderson said on Twitter: 'He's done so much for this England team not just as captain but also as a player. He will be missed but he hands over to a very fine replacement in Alastair Cook.'
>
> His former England team-mate Paul Collingwood tweeted: 'Andrew Strauss should be very proud of what he's done for English cricket and everything he's achieved, great team man and great leader.'
>
> Strauss led his country in 50 of his 100 Tests, including home and away Ashes victories over Australia. He was England's third most experienced captain, and the second most successful, behind Michael Vaughan.
>
> But his retirement comes in the wake of dressing room unrest which led to the axing of batsman Kevin Pietersen from the side.

Cook scored a century in his Test debut against India in 2006, and cemented his reputation during England's Ashes campaign in Australia in 2010-11, scoring 766 runs at an average of 127.

Former England opener Michael Atherton said: 'He was a very good captain held in very high regard by his team, and that is critical. He led in a manner that has gone down well with the public at large.'

Weaving in the background

An important news story will draw on a wide range of sources and include a lot of background detail and analysis. All of this must be structured logically and flow smoothly. To avoid interrupting the flow of the story with chunks of background detail, this should, where possible, be woven into the breaking news, as we saw on p.75.

Example

The 35-year-old Middlesex batsman has ended his three-and-a-half-year reign as England's Test captain, and retired from all forms of cricket.

He said: 'It hasn't been something that occurred overnight. It has built over a few months. I would like to go out on my own terms with my head held high and I think this is the right time.'

This sentence provides a lot of background information (Strauss plays for Middlesex, he is 35 years old and he captained the team for three-and-a-half years) which some readers will need to be told if they are to understand the story fully. But it is used unobtrusively (as an alternative means of referring to Strauss) to introduce a fresh quote, so readers who are familiar with Strauss's background will not feel they are being given a lot of information they already know.

Weaving background information into the body of the story in this way avoids any impression of talking down to the reader. It is often difficult, particularly with sports stories, to gauge how much knowledge readers already have. Keen cricket followers will know much of the background to this story already, but many readers may not. Slipping it into the story in this way helps to disguise the fact that some readers are being fed a lot of unnecessary background. It also means that, although the story has a rigid structure, it is not apparent to the reader, who merely sees a smooth flow of copy. The structure of a news story only becomes apparent to the reader if it is confusingly written.

Of course, some newspapers may now choose to display this background information in separate panels in the manner many readers will be familiar with from websites.

WRITING STYLE

Students who are used to writing essays often find other difficulties when they are asked to write news stories for the first time. These usually involve length, style and the admissibility of the writer's own opinions. Essays can be long and opinionated: news stories should be written as concisely as possible, and their writers should keep their opinions to themselves.

A 1500-word essay has the space to allow the writer to be expansive and even florid; a 150-word news story does not. News stories should be written tightly, leaving out superfluous words, stylistic flourishes and unnecessary information. Every word has to earn its place.

Cutting out unnecessary words means that more information can be packed into the story, or more stories can be squeezed into the page. A journalist should always go back over the first draft of a story to see how the writing can be tightened up. It almost always can. Many common phrases can be reduced to a single word, such as 'in order to' (to), 'in the region of' (about), 'despite the fact that' (though), 'in view of the fact that' (because). Avoid tautology such as 'fastest *ever*' and '*final* result', and meaningless descriptive words such as '*pretty* impressive' and '*very* powerful'. Cutting out superfluous words can save a lot of space in a news story.

EXERCISE

Rewrite the following story, reducing it to half the number of words without losing any of the information it contains.

The two teams who will meet to contest the XLVI Super Bowl at Lucas Oil Stadium, Indianapolis, Indiana, on February the 5th have been decided. They will be the New England Patriots and the New York Giants.

The Patriots will enter the game having completed the regular season with a record of 13-3, which is the best ever recorded in the AFC. They are now seeking their fourth Super Bowl win. Meanwhile, the Giants booked their place in the Super Bowl after finishing the regular season with a record of 9-7, the lowest regular season record in the NFC. They, too, are seeking their fourth Super Bowl victory.

In view of the fact that the same two teams played each other in Super Bowl XLII back in 2007, when the New York Giants beat the New England Patriots by a score of 17-14, the Giants may have the psychological edge. However, the New England Patriots have the better record in the Super Bowl this century, having won three times, in 2001, 2003 and 2004.

Suggested answer:

> The New England Patriots will meet the New York Giants in the XLVI Super Bowl at Indianapolis on February 5.
>
> The Patriots, who have already won the Super Bowl three times this century, won the AFC with a best-ever 13-3 record. The Giants finished the NFC season with a 9-7 record, the lowest ever.
>
> Both are looking to win their fourth Super Bowl. The game will be a repeat of Super Bowl XLII which New York won 17-14.

The first story contains 171 words. The second contains only 74. Yet it retains all the facts and is easier to read. The space saved will create room for the writer to develop the story further, or allow the sports editor to get another story on the page.

Keeping it simple

The grammar of a news story should be simple and uncluttered. Complex sentences, with subordinate clauses, should be avoided. Sentences should be short and direct. They should run to 30 words or less, and paragraphs should be no more than two sentences. Longer paragraphs look grey and daunting and difficult to read when set across the narrow columns of a newspaper page (see Chapter 2). Try to avoid clichés and euphemisms, and if one appears in your story, search for an alternative. People don't 'pass away', they die; teams don't 'get a result', they win.

While avoiding euphemisms, you should ensure that the tone of your story is appropriate to the subject matter. Humour can be a useful tool in the writing of some stories, but should be avoided where it might cause distress or offence.

Judging what might offend or distress readers when reporting tragic events such as a stadium disaster or a fatal accident to one of the competitors in a sporting fixture can be difficult. Always bear in mind that the relatives or friends of those involved may be reading what you have written. Stick to the relevant facts, do not go into unnecessarily unpleasant detail (even when this will show how thoroughly you have done your job), avoid sensationalism and resist the temptation to apportion blame or rush to judgement.

Avoid using jargon. Find a way of saying the same thing in plain English. And do not use acronyms without explaining what they mean (MCG – Melbourne Cricket Ground; IOC – International Olympic Committee) unless you are sure your readers will understand them.

In some cases it may be necessary to amplify the official titles of sporting organisations or competitions, especially when some British sports are being covered in non-British media. The British invented or codified many of the world's leading sports, and just as the United Kingdom does not put its name on its stamps because it was the first country to introduce a modern postal system, so many British sports' governing bodies and some of its (and the world's) major sporting events do not include the words British or English in their titles. The body which runs soccer in England is simply The Football Association. Britain's golf 'major' is officially The Open, its tennis grand slam The Championships. The latter is universally known as Wimbledon, but non-British audiences may need to be told that you are referring to the (English) Football Association or the (British) Open golf tournament.

EXERCISE

Rewrite the following story so that it is simpler and easier to read. Remove any clichés, euphemisms and jargon, and explain any acronyms. Remove any of the writer's own opinions or prejudgements, and make sure that nothing in the content or tone of the story will cause unnecessary offence or distress to readers.

F1 is likely to claim another victim today as legendary driver Jim Smith, who was the youngest man ever to win a GP and who, according to many judges, was destined to become world champion, lies in a hospital bed on the verge of death.

The Aussie speed merchant met his Waterloo when, in only his second race in Britain and in weather conditions rarely experienced Down Under, he spun off the Loamshire track and, as the crowd watched in stunned silence, smashed sickeningly into the trackside barriers.

The initial speculation was that the Aussie, who's just 23 and engaged to top pop songstress Sonja Green, who was watching in horror from the stand, had passed away on the spot.

He was rushed to LGH in a chopper, and fans feared he would be pronounced DOA but, much to their relief, medics later declared he was in ITU with a depressed cranium and fractured tibia and scapula.

It was obvious there were two reasons for the incipient fatality, the first being that Bob Black tried an overtaking manoeuvre that would have made a Sunday driver on a wet Bank Holiday look competent, and clipped his rear wheel, while the second was that the powers that be failed to make sure the circuit was fit to race on, with the unacceptable level of oil on the track undoubtedly contributing to the near-fatal skid.

Experts at the HSE have launched a thorough investigation.

Discussion

Several of the paragraphs are far too complex, with sub-clauses that interrupt the flow of the story and inhibit our understanding of it. They should be broken down into shorter sentences, with the less-important supporting information used further down the story.

The writer's assumptions about the likely fate of the driver and the causes of the accident are opinion, not fact. They have no place in a news story (although the opinions of doctors at the hospital or race track officials could be included if they were properly attributed).

The writer's speculation that the driver will die is not supported by any medical opinion and will cause distress to those close to him. When injuries are life-threatening it is better to describe the victims as fighting for their lives.

Initials and acronyms like F1 and HSE should be spelled out, at least in the first instance, as should abbreviations like GP and DOA. Not every reader will know what they mean. The word 'legendary' is misused – a legend is a traditional story, often untrue. Slang like 'speed merchant' and 'Down Under' and clichés like 'met his Waterloo' and 'stunned silence' should be avoided, especially in stories with subject matter as serious as this. Descriptions like 'watched in horror' (how else would his fiancée view the accident?) and 'sickeningly' are unnecessarily sensationalist, while 'top pop songstress' and the reference to Sunday drivers are too flippant to be used in this kind of story.

'Passed away' is a euphemism, and cranium, tibia and scapula are medical terms which should be replaced by the common descriptions. We don't need to be told that the investigation will be thorough: nobody would expect it to be slipshod.

Suggested answer

The Formula 1 racing driver Jim Smith is fighting for his life today after his car spun off the Loamshire circuit and hit crash barriers.

He was taken by helicopter to Loamshire General Hospital, where he is in intensive care suffering from a fractured skull and broken leg and shoulder blade.

The Australian was taking part in his second race in Britain when he spun off in heavy rain. His fiancée, the pop singer Sonja Green, was watching from the stand.

The accident happened when another driver, Bob Black, tried to overtake and seemed to make contact with Smith's rear wheel. The Health and Safety Executive is investigating.

Smith (23) is the youngest man to win a Grand Prix and was regarded as a future world champion.

Stick to the facts

Opinion has no place in a news story. Stick to the facts and let the readers draw their own conclusions from them. When writing a news story, a reporter should always follow the principles of accuracy, objectivity, neutrality, balance and fairness, and make sure that fact is always clearly distinguished from opinion. The only exception to this is if you are writing for a local newspaper covering a local team or individual, or a national newspaper writing about the country's sporting interests. In such cases you will know where the interests of your readers lie and can write the piece from their point of view. But no matter what publication a story is being written for, accuracy, fairness and the separation of fact and opinion remain sacrosanct.

The information on which a sports story (or any other piece of journalism) is based should always be checked carefully. Being 'fairly sure' that what you are saying is accurate is not good enough. Journalists have a duty to their audiences to make sure that what they are saying is correct. They also have a duty to themselves and the organisations they work for to make sure that what they say does not lead to court proceedings. Seemingly trivial inaccuracies can make a story libellous. Minor errors can have expensive consequences.

The facts of a story should always be verified by reliable sources. Never base a story on hearsay evidence or rumour, and no matter how good a story seems to be, do not use it until you have checked it. The most sensational stories are often those which are likely to be inaccurate. Even inconsequential errors of fact can make you look foolish. If you 'think' a sportsman is a Czech and he turns out to be Slovakian, you will not be sued. But the fans of the club for which the Slovakian plays will know you got it wrong, and they will start to doubt the accuracy of everything else you say. It is much safer to check on the Czech. The golden rule you must always follow is: IF IN DOUBT, LEAVE IT OUT.

Similarly, you should never make assumptions without checking that they are correct, no matter how obvious they seem to you. For instance, if a cricketer with a well-documented history of marital difficulties suddenly pulls out of an overseas tour 'for family reasons', it is tempting to assume that his marriage is on the rocks again. Yet it could be that one of his parents or children is seriously ill. Jumping to the wrong conclusion could be extremely insensitive and embarrassing. The dictum to remember is: Never ASSUME – it makes an ASS out of U and ME.

RUNNING STORIES AND FOLLOW-UPS

Some news stories are self-contained. Once we have read them there is nothing more we need to know. But many breaking stories are merely starting points. As time goes by the story will develop, or will have consequences which can lead to follow-up stories being written. Such stories fall into two categories – the RUNNING STORY and the FOLLOW-UP.

A running story is one which develops over time. It may begin with an announcement by a drugs testing agency that an athlete has failed a drugs test, but from that point the story may 'run' for weeks. That announcement will be followed by a statement from the athlete accepting or denying guilt. Once the athlete's club or the sport's governing body has had time to consider the news, it will make a statement about whether the athlete is to be suspended from competition. The governing body will announce when its disciplinary committee will meet to hear the case. Fellow athletes will enter the debate with statements of support or criticism. The hearing will take place, a decision will be announced and a punishment may be imposed. There will be further public debate about whether the decision was just or the punishment is appropriate, and about the effects on the sport. The athlete may appeal against the decision or the punishment. If he or she is an international athlete, there may be consequences for the national team. The appeal will be heard. The national and international governing bodies may change their rules on drugs and drugs testing as a result of the case. A story which began with a simple announcement can often run for weeks or even years.

Follow-ups tend to be more limited in scope, maybe filling in some of the background or looking at the consequences of the original story. For instance, if a player moves from one club to another, a follow-up story may focus on how his original club intends to replace him in the team and what it intends to spend any transfer fee on. Or it could be angled on the role the player will be expected to perform at his new club, and the consequences of his arrival for any of his team-mates there.

Looking for a follow-up to a story can be a useful way of generating copy when there is not much other news around. The news content of many Sunday newspapers can consist largely of follow-ups to that week's news.

JOURNALISTIC ETHICS

Gathering information for and writing sports news stories will inevitably involve questions of journalistic ethics from time to time. It is rarely, if ever, acceptable for a journalist to resort to lies or deception in pursuit of a news story, or to secretly tape or film interviews. (Exceptions have been made when serious wrongdoing has been investigated, but only after careful consideration and consultation with senior news executives.)

Privacy

Issues of privacy are more difficult to handle. Sports men and women are necessarily in the public eye, they are often well rewarded for their skills, and many have been accorded celebrity status by the media. Public interest in them is, therefore, greater than it is in ordinary citizens. That does not, of course, mean that they are not entitled to their privacy, but it does mean that their activities are more closely scrutinised. Indiscretions involving drink or drugs or sex, or illegal activity which might go unnoticed in other people, can become big stories as media organisations compete with each other for fresh revelations. There is an argument that 'sleaze' stories of this kind are in the public interest because the subjects are role models, especially for young people. However, the line between the right to privacy and the public's right to know is a fine one, and many of the discussions about journalistic ethics are around where that line should be drawn. The debate is especially fierce around kiss-and-tell stories, and whether the media should pay for bedroom revelations about sporting celebrities. Does the fact that someone is willing to reveal intimate details of a relationship give the media the right to invade the other partner's privacy?

Contempt of court

The indiscretions of some sports personalities lead to appearances in court. In one sense, this makes the journalist's job easier. Court hearings are public events which the media are entitled to report. Indeed, the involvement of the media is enshrined in the notion that justice should not only be done but should be *seen* to be done. However, the public's thirst for knowledge about celebrities should not tempt journalists to exceed their rights and responsibilities in relation to court proceedings. They need to take special care about what they publish in advance of any trial, or they may find themselves in contempt of court.

In Britain and some other countries, once a person has been charged with an offence there are strict limits about what the media can report before it is mentioned in court. For instance, a case involving the Leeds United footballers Jonathan Woodgate and Lee Bowyer over an incident outside a night club was halted by the Judge and had to be retried after an article appeared in a national newspaper.

Quotes

Direct quotes should never be altered, except in the interests of clarity or to correct an obvious error made by the person being quoted. They should never be edited or condensed without clear acknowledgement, and only then if the sense is unaltered.

Embargoes

An EMBARGO should always be respected, unless it has been imposed with the clear intention of delaying publication of a matter of public interest which would otherwise have appeared in the media earlier. It is common (and perfectly legitimate) for organisations to issue embargoed information to journalists in advance of the time at which it would otherwise have been made public. This gives the media an opportunity to prepare their stories thoroughly and dissuades journalists from publishing incomplete or inaccurate stories in order to avoid being beaten by their competitors. Indeed, most journalists find the embargo system useful, as it avoids the need for an unnecessary competitive scramble and gives them time to seek reaction to the story in advance of publication.

Embargoes are not legally binding, but most journalists abide by them because if they don't, they may fall victim to someone else's embargo-busting in future. However, if a journalist has obtained the same information from another source before the embargoed material arrives, he or she need not feel bound by the embargo. The simple rule with embargoes is to play fair by your journalist colleagues, but not to allow the subsequent release of embargoed material to deny you an EXCLUSIVE you have worked for and obtained through your own contacts.

Sensibilities

Sports journalists should always take care not to offend the sensibilities of others. They should take particular care to avoid sexism, racism, ageism and issues around disability creeping into their writing. The sports people about whom they write are predominantly young, white and male, and it is easy to overlook the interests of people who do not fit into that category.

Recent changes in sport and sports journalism mean that some prejudices are gradually being tackled. There is now more coverage of women's sport, particularly sports like football, cricket and rugby, which have been traditionally associated with men. There are also more female sports writers and presenters, although the balance in both cases is still overwhelmingly male. Similarly, black players and competitors have now established themselves and become successful in most professional sports, though the number of black sports journalists is still quite small.

The problems of racism in sport, and in sports journalism, have not disappeared, however. Racial taunts are still common among some sections of crowds at sporting events, while high-profile incidents involving English Premier League footballers suggest that the problem can spill over into the playing area too. Unguarded remarks made by television commentators on both sides of the Atlantic about black football players show that it has not been entirely eliminated from the media either.

The media still have a tendency to ignore events for disabled people or sports played mainly by older people (such as bowls), or to consign them to their own little ghettoes on the sports pages.

Influence

The relationship between sports journalists and the sports they cover is inevitably a close one. They must never allow it to become incestuous. Journalists are almost always given free access to events. They also get privileged access to competitors, players, coaches and administrators. They are sometimes provided with free travel and accommodation by event organisers or sponsors. They can be entertained or offered gifts of various kinds. All of this is perfectly legitimate, so long as journalists do not allow it to affect their objectivity or inhibit them from critical coverage when it is necessary.

THE ROLE OF THE SPORTS PHOTOGRAPHER

The technical skills of the sports photographer are outside the scope of this book, but photography plays a vital part in the sports coverage of newspapers and websites. Photographers and journalists often work closely together on stories and features, the work of one complementing that of the other.

The role of the sports photographer is a difficult one. It often involves standing out in the cold, at a less-than-perfect vantage point, trying to keep an eye on the action and not miss important incidents like goals, while also looking for the unusual or dramatic picture. The sports photographer will usually be working alone, covering an event on which television may be focusing half a dozen cameras. It is an unequal contest.

For that reason, many photographers do not try to compete with television, which can cover the key moments from a number of different angles. Instead, they try to create their impact through the composition of their pictures and the action taking place in them, the expressions on competitors' faces, the contortions of their bodies, or maybe the flashpoint of an argument between opponents. Sometimes the most telling pictures are taken off the field of play and away from the competitors, concentrating on referees or umpires or the reaction of the crowd.

Most major newspapers employ specialist sports photographers, but many have to double up as news photographers on weekdays, and turn out to sporting events in the evening or on Saturday afternoons. They often face deadlines even tighter than those of their journalist colleagues, though sending pictures back to base is now easier since the arrival of digital cameras. Photographers who, until recently, had to leave an event early and go back to the darkroom to process their pictures can now send them direct from the stadium. They can also preview the images they have taken and select those which work best.

However, like writers, once a photographer's work has been filed, it is out of his or her hands. The final decision about which picture to use will be taken by a page designer or sub-editor. In the end, picture selection will depend on the space available on a page, and whether an upright or portrait shape works better than a landscape. Only in exceptional circumstances will pages be redesigned to accommodate a really good picture.

The digital revolution, however, has vastly increased the opportunities for a sports photographer's work to be seen. Websites have far more space than newspapers in which they can display photographs, and will often choose to tell the story of a major sports event in pictures as well as in words. Many media outlets will also display a range of pictures on social media sites such as Flickr in an attempt to build new audiences and attract them to their own products.

Summary

The ability to research and write news stories are two of the key skills of the sports journalist. News stories are written to a formula, with the key points summarised in the opening paragraph (intro) and elaborated in order of importance in the main body of the story. They should be written so that they can be cut from the bottom to fit whatever space is available and in such a way that they make sense no matter where they are cut. Style and language should be as simple as possible, stories should stick to fact rather than opinion, and they should be accurate and fair to those involved.

8 Sports features

Chapter Summary

- What is a sports feature?
- Finding a 'peg' or angle
- Constructing a feature: intros, the body of the feature and outros or payoffs
- The standfirst
- Profiles
- Opinion columns
- Editorials
- Participation features
- Crossover pieces

WHAT IS A SPORTS FEATURE?

Features are longer pieces of journalism which give writers the opportunity to treat a subject or individual in depth, and often with style and wit. A feature-length article allows more space for background information, contributions from a greater number of sources covering a wider range of issues, and an opportunity to provide more comment and analysis. It also allows the writer to abandon the tight constraints of news story construction and write in a more colourful way. Because features need to sustain the interest of the reader over a longer period – anything from 500 to several thousand words – they need to be written in a bright and entertaining style.

The golden rules for writing features are:

- Grab their attention
- Keep their attention
- Leave them satisfied

FINDING A 'PEG' OR ANGLE

Any piece of journalism needs a subject, but it is not enough simply to write about your favourite athlete or team. There has to be a reason for doing so, to engage the interest of readers. The subject around which a feature is written is normally in the news, or in the public eye, for some reason. An important sporting event may be coming up; a team or athlete may be doing particularly well or especially badly; a coach may have been fired; a player may be involved in a drugs scandal; someone may have been killed or injured at a stadium; a group of fans may have been involved in hooliganism or racist behaviour.

Any of these (and many other) events provide journalists with the subject matter for features. The events on which features are based are known as PEGS – they are the things on which the features are hung.

Having found a peg, the journalist must then find an ANGLE from which to write the piece. In the run-up to a big game, for instance, the feature writer may choose to focus on previous meetings and the rivalry between the two teams, or base the piece around a current or former player who has represented both teams, or look at the action the police are taking to prevent rival fans clashing. News that a coach has been sacked may prompt features about what makes a successful coach, an analysis of which other coaches may be in the firing line or a retrospective look at those who have already been fired this season, and whether a change of coach makes any difference to a team's success. Some journalists even take part in training sessions or competitions to try to give an insider's view of a sporting event.

CONSTRUCTING A FEATURE

The intro

Features are written in a more colourful style than news stories, and the same applies to intros. The function of the intro remains the same – to grab the reader's interest – but this can be done in a wider variety of ways than merely presenting the most important facts. The more expansive form of the feature allows journalists to approach the subject matter in a more subtle manner. Feature writers have come up with a range of ways of engaging the reader's interest and teasing them into reading on. Here are some of them:

Dropped intro

This delays the punch, so that the reader is left wondering who or what is the subject, which is then revealed some way into the feature:

> When he walked through the door of the restaurant in a baggy, slightly crumpled suit, he looked a small, deferential figure, who waited patiently for a waiter to show him to my table. It was difficult to believe that the weight of a nation's expectations would be resting on those slight shoulders.

But tomorrow afternoon, with a pack of 20-stone All-Blacks forwards bearing down on him, scrum half Will Smith will be the calm eye at the centre of the most ferocious storm of the international rugby season.

Quote intro

News stories rarely begin with quotes because they get in the way of the facts, but a powerful quote can be a good way into a feature, painting a picture of the person who is speaking and sketching in some of the background before we meet them:

'When I missed that penalty in the semi-final of the World Cup I knew I had cost my team a place in history. But in an odd way it made me a stronger player, and if the Boss is looking for volunteers to take a penalty again this time, I'll be the first in the queue.'

Historical intro

Some features demand to be set in historical perspective. A news feature on a stadium disaster or a gambling scandal might begin with a retrospective look at other disasters or scandals. Similarly, many sporting achievements assume extra interest because of the other achievements – or lack of them – that preceded them:

Anybody who can remember the last time the Giants won the Cup will qualify for concessionary entry to tomorrow's final, because it is seventy years since they last lifted the trophy.

Contrast intro

Another teasing way into a feature is to make use of any contrasts the subject throws up. This might mean contrasting a giant defender on one team with a small but nippy forward on the other. Or it might be to contrast the past life or fortunes of a participant with the personality who is about to occupy centre stage:

Though he's never played at Wembley Stadium, Mark Jones will feel perfectly at home when he walks on to the pitch. A year ago, as a brickie, he was helping to build the place with trowel and cement: tomorrow, as a pro, he'll be holding another wall together, as the keystone of the United defence.

Question intro

A question would reduce the impact of the intro of a news story, but in a feature a question can again be used to whet the readers' appetites and coax them into discovering the answer:

How much would you pay to see your favourite team get slaughtered? Well, the fans of non-league Gresford Rovers, who normally pay three pounds to see their team's home matches, are willing to pay three hundred pounds for a ticket for their side's visit to the European champions in the next round of the cup.

This is just a selection of the ways in which features can be introduced. What they have in common is that they make the reader sit up and take notice. There are innumerable variations on these themes, and two or more intro types can sometimes be combined. Always read the intros to features carefully and try to work out what the writer is doing and how he or she is luring you into reading the rest of the piece – the main body of the feature.

The body of the feature

Because most features have a news peg, we can almost take the news angle as read – that this pitcher is about to play in the World Series, that this jockey is riding the favourite in the big race, that an athlete has tested positive for drugs in the Olympic Games. The purpose of the body of the feature is to fill in the background to the news angle, by painting pictures of the people involved, by analysing the consequences of a newsworthy event, by trying to predict what will happen in the future. And to maintain the reader's interest over the longer distance, it is important that the writing should be colourful and varied, moving smoothly through a range of elements, from description to quotes to background detail to analysis, with bridging passages to link the various elements. There are examples of all these things later in this chapter.

The outro or payoff

The final paragraph of a news story is the least important, the first to be cut if the piece is too long. But because a feature must strive to maintain the reader's interest to the end, the final paragraph is not expendable. After the intro, it is perhaps the most important in the piece, because it is the one that will leave the final impression on the reader. The last paragraph of a feature is called the OUTRO (the opposite of an intro) or PAYOFF, and should round the piece off in a satisfactory way, just as the final paragraph of a novel does.

There are various ways of achieving this sense of wholeness. One of the most common is to bring the piece full circle, finishing it where it started:

Intro: Stratford striker Steve Strong is no stranger to finding his way through congested areas. His day job is as a bus driver in London's northern suburbs.

Outro: So after ninety minutes trying to find a way through the Liverpool defence, coping with rush hour on the North Circular will seem like child's play.

An analytical piece may end by summarising the arguments it has covered, reach a conclusion or end by asking a question. A profile may end with a telling quote.

The standfirst

To give the reader a flavour of what the piece is about and to add visual interest to the page on which it appears, a feature is often preceded by a STANDFIRST. This is a short paragraph which outlines the thrust of the piece. It usually contains the writer's byline. Although it is the first thing (other than the headline) most people will read, it tends to be the last thing to be written, and will often be provided by a sub-editor rather than the journalist who wrote the piece.

Example

The Olympic Games return to their birthplace this year, but the facilities may not be ready on time. Summer spectacular or Greek tragedy? **Barbara Brown** reports from Athens.

PROFILES

The most common form of feature found on the sports pages is the PROFILE. A profile is a biographical piece on an athlete, coach or administrator who is currently in the news. A profile can be as short as a few paragraphs or can fill a couple of pages. By definition, it is a human-interest story, often with a celebrity at its heart, and therefore doubly popular with readers.

As explained above and in Chapter 6, the peg on which a profile is hung will often be the subject's involvement in an important forthcoming sports event. The piece will be written as part of the build-up to the event and the subject chosen because, of all the players taking part, he or she is of particular interest. The person may have played for the opposing team at some stage in the past, or be in a rich streak of form, or on the verge of breaking some sort of record, such as the number of goals or points or runs scored in the competition.

The most common way of gathering information for a profile is to interview the subject, and get his or her views on the forthcoming events and on the strengths and weaknesses of his or her own and the opposing team. (Interview techniques are covered in Chapter 5.) But the best profiles, particularly those which aim to present a rounded picture of the subject rather than simply to elicit the person's views on a particular event, will look wider than this. They will also include the views of team-mates or opponents who know him or her, coaches who have worked with the person and can assess his or her strengths and weaknesses, and background information on the subject's past achievements. This is one reason why a sports journalist needs a wide range of contacts.

If you can't get an interview with the subject of your profile (and it can be extremely difficult to arrange a one-to-one interview with leading sports personalities), it is possible to obtain their views from other sources. Many are contractually bound to attend press conferences before or after the events in which they are taking part, when you may be able to put some of your questions. Quotes they have made previously can be obtained from cuttings or online archives, and many have their own websites and social media sites, on which they give their views about a range of issues. When using material from these sources, however, you should take care not to infringe copyright laws (see Appendix 2).

Example

The following is a profile of the American golfer Tiger Woods. The paragraphs are numbered for ease of reference in the discussion which follows.

1 Nobody's been paying much attention to the man who's been stealthily creeping up the world golf rankings for the past year.

2 For those whose main interest in the sport is the Major tournaments, his name has usually appeared well down the Leader Board.

3 But elsewhere on the circuit, he's been steadily accumulating victories, with three to his name this season.

4 And while the world's attention has been on the succession of Brits jostling for position as World No 1, the American has quietly moved up from 58th to second in the rankings.

5 Yes, Tiger Woods is back.

6 The former undisputed king of golf has been making the headlines for all the wrong reasons since that notorious late-night collision with a fire hydrant nearly three years ago.

7 Loss of reputation, loss of sponsors and loss of wife and children led to a disastrous loss of form, and after years as No 1, he dropped out of the top 50.

8 But now, after those long years in the wilderness, he's back to No 2 in the world. In December Woods won the Chevron World Challenge, his first win for more than two years, and has followed that up with two more.

9 So will Tiger be burning bright at golf's highest-profile event, the Ryder Cup, which starts in Chicago on Friday?

10 Woods has never shone in the Ryder Cup, which the United States will be trying to wrest from the grasp of the Europeans at the Medinah Club. He has played in six and been on the winning side only once. Of the 29 matches he has played, he has won only 13 times – four in the singles.

11   He recognises his past failings as a team player, but is confident that all that is now behind him. 'I didn't earn the points that I was put out there for,' he says.

12   'I believe I was out there in five sessions each time and I didn't go 5-0 on our side. So I certainly am a part of that and that's part of being a team. I needed to go get my points for my team, and I didn't do that. Hopefully I can do that this week and hopefully the other guys can do the same and we can get this thing rolling.'

13   Before his fall from grace, Woods' presence in the US team was not always positive. Because he was so successful as an individual – he has won 14 Majors – many felt he never committed fully to the team.

14   His reputation overwhelmed his fellow players, and few of them could get on with him. Then, after the hydrant incident and the revelations of multiple infidelities which followed, his confidence had gone.

15   'I think he realises he was trying too hard when he broke into the team,' says Davis Love III, captain of the US team. 'He couldn't do it all by himself. He had to be part of the team and win points with his partners.'

16   'It means a lot to him. He has asked me 50 questions in the last two years, and 48 of them have been about the Ryder Cup.'

17   Before his fall from grace, which led to lurid media coverage of nights in hotel rooms with a succession of women, the loss of major sponsors such as AT&T, Gatorade and General Motors, and his eventual divorce from his Swedish model wife Elin Nordegren, he'd been in a league of his own.

18   He has won 71 tournaments and £93 million, way ahead of any other player in the history of the game. And that may have contributed to his poor performances in the Ryder Cup, where his body language – hunched shoulders and hangdog expression – often suggested he didn't want to be there.

19   Europe's Graeme McDowell, who secured the winning point for his team at Celtic Manor two years ago, believes that in the six Ryder Cup competitions he's played in, Woods was often the victim of 'lesser' players raising their game and playing without pressure.

20   'It's a huge game for an underdog to play a Tiger Woods. They get up for it. They are not expected to win. When expectation levels drop, your game tends to improve. A guy who plays Tiger Woods, or a player of that calibre, doesn't expect to win so he lets it all go and he plays out of his skin and gets the upset.'

21   But Woods, who hasn't won a Major now for five years, may not face that problem this week. Instead, the burden has probably shifted to McDowell's Northern Ireland compatriot and current world No 1, Rory McIlroy, who is the man all the Americans will want to beat.

(Continued)

(Continued)

22 But his record this season shows Woods is well on the way back to his former pre-eminence. He finished third in the Open at Royal Lytham & St Annes and followed up his Chevron victory by winning the Arnold Palmer Invitational in March and the Memorial Tournament in Dublin, Ohio, to equal Jack Nicklaus' record of 73 PGA tour wins.

23 'To do it aged 36 is not too shabby. I've been very proud of what I've done so far. I feel I've got a lot of good years ahead of me,' said Woods.

24 And when cross-pond rivalries resume in Chicago on Friday, he'll be happy for someone else to hog the limelight if it means he can complete his rehabilitation in the one competition in which he has never fulfilled his potential.

Discussion

Paragraph 1: The introduction grabs the attention because it is written in a teasing way. We don't yet know who the piece is about, but we are given just enough information to make us start thinking and want to read on. This is an example of a *dropped intro*.

Paragraphs 2–4: These maintain the suspense, but offer a few more clues to the identity of the subject, and at the same time give us some more background information about him, preparing us for:

Paragraph 5: 'Yes, Tiger Woods is back.' This brief sentence finally lets us in on the secret, and the dropped intro with which the piece begins is complete.

Paragraph 6: This reminds us how highly regarded Woods once was and why he has been out of the limelight. Having jogged our memories, it now refers to the widely publicised moment when Woods drove his car into a fire hydrant outside his home after an argument with his wife. By simply referring to the hydrant, and letting the reader fill in the gaps from his or her own memory, the writer is playing on the reader's pride in his own knowledge of the sport.

Paragraph 7: This now sums up what the reader has just been thinking, but in a very polished way which plays on repeated use of the word 'loss'. 'Loss of reputation, loss of sponsors and loss of wife and children led to a disastrous loss of form....' This is immediately followed by the opposite of such florid writing – two stark, hard facts which concisely sum up the consequences of that notorious evening.

Paragraph 8: This is the fulcrum of the piece. Having knocked down Tiger Woods' reputation, the writer now starts building it up again with a list of his achievements this year. That leads naturally into the next.

Paragraph 9: This introduces the peg for the entire piece – the reason why we are hearing about Tiger Woods again now. He is about to represent the United States again in golf's most prestigious international tournament, the Ryder Cup. And the writer throws in another piece of polished writing designed to entertain the reader and maintain his or her interest – a well-known quotation from William Blake's famous poem *The Tyger*. This again gives the reader a sense of satisfaction at his or her own flash of recognition at this literary reference, and inserting a question into a profile is a useful way of holding the reader's interest.

Paragraph 10: The question leads us smoothly and naturally into the details of the player's record in that competition.

Paragraphs 11 and 12: Having introduced the subject of the profile, we now hear directly from him. Clearly, it is important to quote the subject of a profile if possible. It can be difficult to get a one-to-one interview with leading sports figures because of the demands on their time, but in the run-up to major events such as the Ryder Cup they are often made available to the media by the organisers, who want to maximise publicity for the event. It is media conferences such as these which often provide the core material for such profiles.

Paragraphs 13 and 14: Here the writer uses his own expert knowledge of the sport to analyse what Woods has just said and put his own interpretation on it.

Paragraphs 15 and 16: Good profiles will present a rounded picture by looking at the subject from as many angles as possible. Having heard from the subject, we are now offered the opinion of someone who knows him well and has detailed inside knowledge of the issues the piece has just been discussing – the team's captain.

Paragraphs 17 and 18: Moving frequently from narrative to quotation and back to narrative again helps maintain the reader's interest, and here the writer switches focus again to fill in a little more of the story's background and paint a little word-portrait of the subject. Unlike a radio or television interview, in print we can't see or hear the person who is talking. But a person's body language and general demeanour often helps us interpret what they are saying and helps paint a picture of the person in our minds. The reader, therefore, needs to be told.

Paragraphs 19 and 20: Now we move back to quotation, and a view from someone else who can give an expert opinion on Woods – one of his opponents. In introducing McDowell, the writer also unobtrusively slips in a bit more information about Woods, Ryder Cup record.

Paragraphs 21 and 22: The piece returns to narrative mode again and begins to form its conclusion, with detail about the player who has taken over at the top of the world rankings, and an appraisal of Woods' current form.

Paragraph 23: The focus switches to quotation again, bringing us back to the person we first heard from – Woods himself.

Paragraph 24: The outro, or payoff, neatly bring the piece full circle. It picks up the reference in the intro to Woods being out of the limelight. Referring back to the intro in this way is a useful device because it leaves the reader with the feeling of having read a carefully crafted, rounded piece that ends satisfactorily rather than merely petering out.

OPINION COLUMNS

Opinion columns are useful components of the sports pages for a number of reasons. They help to fill the space on those quiet days when there is not much live sport on which to report; they give an opportunity for the paper's best journalists to write with style and wit; they offer a platform to well-known figures from the world of sport, whose names above their columns will attract readers; they generate controversy and provoke discussion and argument among readers; and they help to keep running stories alive until the next significant development crops up. These things are particularly important now that many people get their basic information – especially about sport – from sources other than newspapers, such as radio, television, social network sites and websites.

Columnists range from those with regular weekly slots to those who write an opinion piece only when the spirit moves them or when they are specially commissioned to do so because of their unique expertise. They include former sports professionals and coaches who can bring their first-hand experience to the stories of the day, and the best sports journalists, who enliven the pages with stylish, witty, entertaining and controversial writing.

The best opinion columns combine the insights of the sports expert and the style of the professional writer. Opinion columns should be informed, but they should also be well-constructed pieces of writing. Columns can be made up of a single, longer piece or a number of shorter items.

As with most other features, an opinion column needs a peg on which it can be hung. The peg will often be a current story with an element of controversy to it – a failed drugs test, an outburst by a coach, a change to the rules of a sport – that will give the writer the opportunity to explore all sides of the issue and come down on one side or the other. Many columns are the printed equivalent of a discussion in the pub or on the way home from the game.

The most important element of a good column is controversy. The writer's opinions don't have to be popular, or even reflect the views of the paper for which he or she is writing. Some of the best columnists deliberately take unpopular views to stimulate the readers' interest and give them something to argue against. But opinions should always be based on hard facts, so careful research is essential. And an opinion column should never be used to pursue grudges.

People don't read columns primarily for information, although a good column will supply its readers with all the information they need to understand it and the arguments advanced in it. They read them for the views expressed and the quality and entertainment value of the writing. So an effective column, like any other feature, will need to grab the reader's attention from the outset and hold it through to the end. Ideally, it will also leave readers with a sense of satisfaction and encourage them to read more by the same writer the next time the column appears.

An effective column will probably need some, though not necessarily all, of the following elements:

A peg – a recent news story with an element of controversy on which the piece is based.

An arresting intro which will engage the readers' attention and make them want to read on (see notes on intros above).

A witty, controversial, no-nonsense, hard-hitting style with vocabulary, grammar and sentence-length appropriate to the paper for which it is written.

An insider's view or expert analysis of the issue, airing all sides of the argument and making comparisons with other people or events, if necessary.

A definite stance, with arguments which justify your position.

A recap of the story and any background detail necessary to allow readers to understand the piece. A judgement may be needed as to how much knowledge the reader can be expected to bring to the piece. If it uses a major sports story as its peg, the reader will probably be familiar with the basic detail.

An ending which will leave readers with the feeling they have read a well-rounded and satisfying piece.

Elements of an opinion column

- Find a peg
- Write an arresting intro
- Recap the story
- Give any necessary background detail
- Make comparisons, if necessary
- Give both sides of the argument
- Reach a conclusion
- Justify it
- Write with wit, humour and style
- Be controversial
- End in a satisfying way

Example

The following is an opinion piece about women being admitted to one of the world's top golf clubs for the first time. The peg is a short news item. The paragraphs are numbered for ease of reference in the discussion which follows.

News item

For the first time in its 80-year history, Augusta National Golf Club has female members.

(Continued)

(Continued)

The home of The Masters golf championship, which has faced increasing criticism because of its all-male membership, has invited former US secretary of state Condoleezza Rice and South Carolina financier Darla Moore to become members.

They will become the first women to wear the club's famous green jacket when the new season opens in October.

Opinion piece

1 So former US secretary of state Condoleezza Rice and South Carolina financier Darla Moore are being measured up for green jackets.

2 Augusta National Golf Club, home to The Masters tournament, has finally admitted female members for the first time in its 80-year history.

3 So that's all right, then, and all is now well in the formerly sexist world of golf.

4 If only that were so.

5 Of course, it is a small step forward that the home of one of the four Majors has finally joined the 21st century, albeit with a gun to its head. And it has taken some time. The club was founded 80 years ago.

6 Former club chairman Hootie Johnson once famously said that Augusta National would not allow women in 'at the point of a bayonet.' But the arms race has intensified since then.

7 Earlier this year, presidential candidates Barack Obama and Mitt Romney both condemned the club's stance on women's membership. (Well, you wouldn't want to alienate 50 per cent of voters in election year, would you?)

8 So now we've reached the point where the club with enough nice flowerbeds to attract hundreds of women members can't resist the pressure any longer.

9 And like any other organisation forced on to the back foot, they're conceding ground an inch at a time. Or, to use a term more familiar in another context in the Deep South, they're trying a little tokenism.

10 It would be nice to think that the admission of a couple of well-heeled and well-connected women, one black and one white, will open the gates to many more women, blacks, or even working-class white males. But I doubt if it will be any time soon.

11 And meanwhile, elsewhere in the world of golf, it's still the 19th century.

12 Across the pond in Scotland, where the game began, the Royal and Ancient at St Andrews, the game's governing body, is still an all-male preserve. And clubs around the world still fiercely protect their men-only bars, and rules which don't allow women on the course until after 10 on Saturdays.

13 Of course, it's easy to see why men would want to keep women out of their clubs. They might inhibit them from telling sexist jokes at the 19th hole.

14 Or they might turn up on the course wearing shorts or other unsuitable items of clothing (as opposed to the chequered trousers and ridiculous baseball caps favoured by middle-aged golfers of the male persuasion).

15 And worst of all, a woman might beat them at golf.

16 My guess is that fair play for the fair sex on the fairways is still a fair way off, despite Augusta National's historic decision.

17 But how many women have ever wanted one of those green jackets anyway? They're not even a good look on men. Condoleezza and Darla may prefer to stick with Armani.

Discussion

Paragraph 1: The intro teases readers into wondering why a reference to a politician in a green jacket should be of interest to them. The peg has not yet been made clear.

Paragraph 2 lets them in on the secret and establishes the connection with sport. It also fills in some of the background to the story and reminds them of the long-running controversy surrounding women's membership of the club.

Paragraphs 3 and 4: The writer gives us the first indication of his ironic view on the story.

Paragraphs 5 and 6 maintain the tone of ironic humour that runs through the piece and defines the writer's style. They fill in more of the background and end with a play on words which pulls together the earlier references to guns and bayonets.

Paragraphs 7 and 8 widen the debate and provide a sardonic explanation for the club's decision.

Paragraphs 9–12 make the serious points of the opinion column and place the story firmly in the wider context of attitudes towards women in world golf; they are now free from irony.

Paragraphs 13–15 return to the style of ironic humour which categorises the piece and helps maintain the reader's interest.

Paragraph 16: A memorable line which uses the word 'fair' in four different ways in a single sentence. Passages of striking writing like this help maintain the reader's interest to the end of the piece.

Paragraph 17 returns to the subject with which the piece started – the green jackets – which rounds the piece off satisfactorily.

NEWS FEATURES

As we have seen in the previous chapter, sport generates news stories beyond the confines of the field of play. They may concern administrators, or finance, or sports arenas, or the organisation of tournaments, or drug abuse, or a host of other things. News features look beyond the bare bones of these stories and expand on them. They may contain description, comment, analysis, background historical detail and eye-witness accounts, and make use of a broader range of sources.

The standfirst quoted above refers to a news feature about preparations for the Olympic Games. The feature would have looked at the delays in building facilities, the reasons for the delays and the likely impact on the competition, and would have quoted Olympic organisers, the host government, national athletics federations and individual athletes. The journalist may also have offered his or her own analysis and synthesis of the evidence gathered for the feature.

EDITORIALS

Sport has now assumed such a central role in modern culture that some of the stories it generates are regarded as serious enough to warrant editorial comment in our newspapers. Editorials (or leaders, or leading articles, as they are sometimes called) reflect the views of the newspaper and are usually carried in a column on the Leader page, with the newspaper's masthead at the top. They can be humorous if the subject allows it, but they are usually serious and reflective, looking at all sides of a story and forming an opinion based on solid argument. They do not seek to provoke controversy for its own sake, as some opinion columns do, but to represent the considered stance of the publication. They are usually written by editorial writing specialists with no BYLINE because these are the considered views of the newspaper.

TIMELESS FEATURES

Occasional gaps in the sporting programme create a demand for pieces that can be used to fill space when few events are taking place and when there are no major stories to provide pegs for feature writers. Because they can be used any time, they are known as TIMELESS PIECES. They may provide an opportunity to look at minority sports which do not normally command space on the sports pages, or to find unusual angles on major ones. Examples of timeless features might be a look at the lives of club mascots or the work of the people who look after the grounds or the playing kit.

COLOUR PIECES

Writers will sometimes be sent to sporting events not to cover the event itself but to give an impression of what it is like to be there. The features they produce are known as COLOUR PIECES, and they are often written from the perspective of the ordinary spectator rather than participant or privileged journalist. Writing a colour piece may involve travelling on the coach with the fans, drinking in a bar with them before the game, walking to the ground with them through the streets of a strange city, joining in the chanting and singing before the game, feeling the elation and the deflation with them as the action unfolds, and dissecting the experience with them afterwards as they make their way home. Colour pieces concentrate on description, on eye-witness reporting, on quotation and on factual detail to give the flavour of being there.

PARTICIPATION FEATURES

Some of the best sports colour features are written by reporters who find out from the inside what it is like to be a sports professional, who join in the training sessions and try to do it themselves. Such pieces attempt to get beyond the surface description of sports events and try to get inside the lives of professional athletes, the training routines, the tactical talks, the treatment tables, and the pain through which they have to push their bodies to succeed. They try to peer beneath the tip of the iceberg that is competition and examine the huge chunks of an athlete's life which lie below the glittering surface.

They also provide an opportunity of 'showing' readers what an athlete's life is like rather than merely 'telling' them. 'Telling' and 'showing' are important weapons in a writer's armoury, and 'showing' is the more powerful. To show someone something is the next best thing to letting them experience it for themselves. To tell someone something is to give them the information second-hand.

Example

1 'Take one of these,' says Chris Walker as we ride out of the car park, 'in case you feel the Knock.'

2 'The what?'

3 'The Knock. We sometimes call it the Bonk.'

4 'I see.'

5 'One of these' is a banana, and the Knock or the Bonk, according to taste, turns out to be the cyclist's equivalent of the Wall, that sudden drop in blood sugar levels that hits athletes after a couple of hours of hard physical effort. You feel the Knock quite often when you take life at an average speed of 30mph, 100 miles a day, seven days a week, 40 weeks a year.

6 Chris Walker is a professional cyclist. He's about to set off on Britain's toughest sporting event, the 14-day, 1150-mile Round Britain Race, and he's invited me along for a spot of last-minute training.

(Continued)

(Continued)

7 Dressed in black ballet tights and a technicolour jersey constructed entirely of sponsors' logos and pockets for my bananas, I am about to discover first-hand (or perhaps through a different part of my anatomy) the pains and pleasures of life in the saddle.

8 We turn left out of the car park, which is just as well, because turning right would have taken us on a 90-mile round-trip through the mountains that Chris has already made twice this week.

9 'Just a nice, steady run,' he says, but we settle instead for a more leisurely 15-mile circuit that will let me get the feel of the ten-gear, £1500, individually tailored, hand-made bike on which Chris spends most of his working life.

10 He's a member of the Raleigh-Banana team, so called because Raleigh make bikes and high-carbohydrate bananas make them go further, releasing a steady flow of energy to the rider over a long race.

11 They make a change from jam and cheese sandwiches, the other big favourites with men on the move.

12 Chris trains up to 500 miles a week in these hills, on the roads and on mountain bikes up almost vertical slopes I would hesitate to tackle with crampons and an ice axe.

13 He has to. A professional cyclist's job security depends on performance, and performance depends on the effort you are prepared to make in training.

14 Top men like Chris make a good living as sponsored riders here and on the Continent, but the less-successful pros, who could earn more for considerably less effort on a building site, are desperate to beat the big names and grab their places in the sponsored teams.

15 'We have to be on the ball all the time,' says Chris, who is 24 and in his third season as a pro. 'The pressure is always on me to do well.'

16 But the really big money comes with winning a place in a team in the Tour de France, arguably the world's greatest sporting event.

17 'I wouldn't want to be a *domestique*, one of the men the Continental teams employ just to help their top men win. I like a bit of glory,' says Chris.

18 But winning bike races depends less on individual riders than on team tactics. The riders in form will have the rest of the team working for them, helping to close up breakaways by other teams, getting them into position for bunch sprints at the end of a stage, and keeping them out of the wind.

19 The rider in the wind at the front of the race uses 30 to 40 per cent more energy than those behind him, which is why races form a peloton, an arrowhead formation with little wind resistance, like a great animal on the move.

20 It is a system open to jealousy and friction among a small group of riders living out of saddlebags for weeks at a time, but strife is rare.

21 'There can be a bit of elbowing and barging in a race,' says Chris. 'It has been known for people to have fights, but it is an unwritten rule that you make up straight away. You have got to ride with these blokes again, week in and week out.'

22 Each team is a mix of sprinters, like Chris, who are good on the flat stages, and climbers, who are good in the mountains. The best climbers are usually tall, light men with a good power-to-weight ratio.

23 At the foot of a hill your tall, light reporter has begun to feel the Knock. I unzip my banana. It is not a good move.

24 To begin with, eating and pedalling a bike uphill are not mutually compatible activities; secondly, it is bad tactics, and tactics are as important in cycling as pedal-power.

25 'If I made an attack on you now, you wouldn't be able to breathe with your mouth full. I would be away,' says Chris. 'You should have eaten before we got to the hill.'

26 'Cycling is like chess on wheels. You have to use a bit of kidology, pretend you are on your last legs all the way up the hill, then shoot past the others at the last minute when there is no chance they will come back at you.'

27 Ten miles into our run, quadriceps complaining at every turn of the crank, 'on the rivet' as we aficionados say (nose right down on the rivet of the handlebars with fatigue), I am happy just to get to the summit.

28 But at least I have discovered why they do it: it's so good when it stops.

29 'It's mind-blowing sometimes. They say marathon running is hard. They run 26 miles perhaps four times a year. We have 100-mile stages every day for a week, and that is just one race,' says Chris.

30 'But if you can wake up every day happy to do it again, that's the difference between a winner and a loser.'

Discussion

Paragraph 1: The piece takes us straight inside the world of professional cycling by introducing us to some of the jargon the professionals, like those in any other business, use among themselves. This is also a good example of a 'dropped intro'. We are not quite sure what is going on until paragraph 6.

Paragraph 5: The physiological effects of the sport and the stark statistics of the mileage a cyclist covers each year are juxtaposed to underline how tough the life can be.

Paragraphs 7 and 8: These paint a word picture of what is happening, undercut by humour to emphasise that the writer is not really part of that world.

Paragraphs 9–10: A lot of thought has gone into the style of the piece. The quote, 'Just a nice steady run', has been chosen for its irony, and the name of the racing team – Raleigh–Banana – has been cleverly deconstructed: 'Raleigh make bikes and high-carbohydrate bananas make them go further.'

Paragraphs 13–16: Having grabbed the attention of the reader in the first few paragraphs, the writer can now free-wheel for a while and throw in some analysis of the realities of a cyclist's life.

Paragraph 17: More insider talk about *domestiques*, but it is explained for the benefit of the outsider, who in this case is the reader.

Paragraph 21: Vivid quotes from the professional build on the earlier descriptions of life behind the scenes.

Paragraphs 23–25: The writer steps back into the picture to 'show' us how the professional's inside knowledge is superior to that of the amateur.

Paragraphs 26–29: The piece ends with more 'shop' jargon, more insider description and quotes, and more humour: 'I have discovered why they do it: it's so good when it stops.'

Paragraph 30: The outro, or payoff, brings us full circle with another quote from the pro – and a telling one which sums up the whole philosophy of the professional bike rider.

EXERCISE

Find a colleague who plays a sport with which you are not familiar. It does not have to be to professional standards. Go to a training session and join in. Talk to the other participants and find out what interests them about the sport and why they do it.

Immediately afterwards, make notes about the experience, of how it felt physically, of how difficult it was to pick up the skills, and jot down any interesting quotes you were given. Write a participatory piece using some of the techniques described in this chapter. Try to make the language you use interesting and amusing; remember that it is better to 'show' than to 'tell', and pay particular attention to the intro and outro.

If you are part of a group, read your pieces to each other and identify those sections which give the best insider's view of the sport. Also try to identify good examples of writing which 'show' us what the sport is about.

CROSSOVER PIECES

Because professional sports people are in the public eye and often highly paid, their activities on and off the field of play are scrutinised with the same interest journalists and their audiences devote to celebrities in any other walk of life. We are interested not only in their work, but also in their private lives. We want to know about their relationships, their health, their leisure activities, their clothes, their sexual misdemeanours, their gambling or drugs or drinking problems, their brushes with the law.

As a result, news stories about sports people will sometimes 'cross over' from strictly sporting topics to other areas of life. These stories often provide pegs for features about social issues. These are known as CROSSOVER PIECES.

For example, shortly before the soccer World Cup finals, the England team captain, David Beckham, damaged the metatarsal bones in his foot. Because the World Cup is one of the biggest sporting events in the world, and Beckham was one of the highest-profile players, the story quickly expanded beyond the confines of the sports pages. For several days, news bulletins and features pages were carrying pieces by doctors and health correspondents, describing the nature of the injury, how such injuries happened and how long it might take to heal. The articles were often accompanied by drawings showing where the metatarsal bones are located. A sports story had crossed over to become a medical story.

Many crossover pieces deal with moral issues, often suggested by court cases or police investigations involving sports stars. Allegations of sexual assault made against footballers in a Welsh hotel prompted pieces about standards of sexual morality in modern sport. Suggestions that Pakistani cricketers had been involved with bookmakers produced pieces about match fixing in cricket and other sports. Allegations about the use of performance-enhancing drugs among cyclists, baseball players and athletes frequently produce pieces examining the role of drugs in sport. An allegation that a referee had used 'inappropriate' language towards a black player led to features about racism in sport.

Such pieces often demand expertise which is outside the field of the sports journalist. They are therefore often written by, or in conjunction with, specialists in other fields, such as medical or business or legal correspondents. Sports journalists are often happy to let other specialists deal with the more controversial off-field issues, to avoid souring relationships with performers they will frequently have to deal with again over sporting issues.

E⟩(ERCISE

Look through the sports pages of your daily newspaper and try to identify stories which lend themselves to crossover pieces. They will normally raise questions about wider social issues. Decide on the angle you would take if you were writing such a piece, and on the other specialist journalists you would collaborate with (or to whom you would hand over the story).

Keep an eye out for crossover pieces in newspapers and magazines. Because their subject matter is often of interest to a very wide readership, they will often appear in the news or features sections of newspapers rather than on the sports pages.

ONLINE FEATURES

All the above advice is equally valid to features carried on websites or as blogs. Unlike newspapers, where space is limited, a website offers limitless space, but that should not be seen as an invitation to write wordy features. In fact, the opposite is true. Website users have come to expect information in a quick and easily digestible form, and they prefer it to come in small segments. The flexibility offered by a website means that feature-length pieces can be structured differently, with a core textual narrative supplemented by quotes displayed separately and with a picture of the person being quoted, or presented in the form of an audio or VIDEO CLIP. Background information can be displayed in graphic form or in SIDEBARS, as we shall see in Chapter 10. There is, of course, no limit on the number of pictures with which you can illustrate an online feature, and this can be a useful and attractive element on a website.

Summary

Sports features serve a number of important functions in newspapers and magazines. Their extended length allows journalists to deal with their subjects in greater depth. It gives them an opportunity to handle their material in a more amusing and creative way, and thus provide readers with the entertainment for which many of them say they turn to in the sports pages. They also offer an opportunity for analysis and opinion, which is normally excluded from 'hard' news stories. But feature writing demands skills as disciplined as those required for reporting sports events or writing news stories. The best way of acquiring them is to study and try to imitate the techniques that professional sports-feature writers bring to their work.

9 Broadcast media

Chapter Summary

- The special demands of broadcast journalism
- The language of broadcasters
- Radio and television sports departments
- What radio and television sports journalists do
- A day in the life of a broadcast sports journalist
- Story structure
- Writing and performing scripts
- Broadcast interviews
- The rights to sports events
- Outside broadcasts
- Commentary
- Research and preparation
- Radio commentary
- Television commentary

Learning Objectives

- To appreciate the importance of sport to the broadcast media
- To recognise the special demands of radio and television
- To identify the elements of radio and television journalism
- To be able to use the language of broadcast journalism
- To be able to write and perform scripts
- To learn the techniques of broadcast interviews
- To recognise the constraints imposed by the rights to broadcast sporting events
- To master the skills of sports commentary in radio and television
- To understand how live sporting events are broadcast

As we have seen in Chapter 2, sport has helped to define the nature of twenty-first-century broadcasting. It has spawned new radio stations and television channels; it is a major factor in the sale of satellite and cable television subscriptions; and countless websites in every developed country of the world have been built around it.

In turn, radio, television and the internet have helped to raise the profile of sports, to turn many clubs into major businesses and players and athletes into millionaires. In return for the money which the sale of rights to broadcast sporting events has brought, sports organisations have adapted to the needs of the broadcasters, particularly of television. They have changed the starting times of events to fit in with television scheduling, they stage their events on many more days of the week, and in some cases – rugby league in England being the best example – have even altered the season in which the sport is played. Television has changed the kit worn by performers – and not merely by encouraging a plethora of advertising logos. One-day cricket matches, for instance, are now played in brightly coloured suits rather than the traditional whites for the benefit of television. In some cases, the rules have been changed, too. American football games are played in short segments to meet the demands of television channels for frequent commercial breaks.

So the fortunes of sports and the broadcasters who cover them are inextricably linked. The need to build and maintain audiences is changing the way television, in particular, covers sport. Broadcasters have moved on from merely pointing the camera at the action. Sports coverage – especially of lengthy events like Test match cricket – now offers much more explanation about the sport in an attempt to broaden the knowledge of viewers and maintain their interest over the longer period. The arrival of digital television now permits viewers to be 'interactive', to use their remote control buttons to tailor sports coverage to their own wishes, and choose to watch individual players or action replays at will. And texts and social media mean that viewers and listeners can now contribute their own opinions to the coverage.

Despite all this, the coverage of sport by the broadcast media remains similar to that of newspapers in many ways. When radio and television were in their infancy, most of the journalists working in these new media had come from newspapers and brought their approach to sport with them. Like newspapers, the broadcast media offer a combination of sports news, previews of sporting events, coverage of those events, features on sports issues and profiles of people in the sporting world. But radio, television and social media all have their unique demands, their own advantages and limitations, which impose specific working practices and different techniques on the journalists who cover sport for them.

THE LANGUAGE OF BROADCASTERS

Print journalists have only words with which to work. These are sometimes supplemented by still photographs, line drawings or other images, but the language of print is the written word. Print journalists may use words in a number of ways – to write stories, headlines, STANDFIRSTS or captions – but, essentially, words are the only tools they have at their disposal.

This is not true of broadcast journalists. Words remain important, and the ability to write well, to be both concise and entertaining, are vital for the broadcast journalist. But, depending on whether they work in radio, television or online, they have a number of other tools available to them which can be combined with words to make up unique, rich and complex languages. The best broadcast journalism uses this diversity of language to the full, as we shall see.

Radio

Elements of radio journalism

It may seem like stating the obvious, but radio is a sound medium. Many people who are new to radio, including experienced journalists who have previously worked in print, forget this, and produce stories which consist entirely of words, as they would for a newspaper.

Words remain the basic building blocks, of course, but the mere act of reading them into a microphone provides an opportunity to impose additional layers of meaning by the use of intonation and emphasis. The journalist's words, however, are merely the starting point for a good piece of radio journalism. The language of radio has other elements.

Radio can transport listeners to the scene of the action by using the sounds they would hear if they were there. Sound is all around us, and nowhere more than at sporting events: the roar of the crowd, the referee's whistle, the starting gun, galloping hooves, racing car engines, oars splashing in water, the sound of bat on ball, announcements over the public address system. When the sound you would hear if you were *actually* at the events is used in radio it is known as ACTUALITY SOUND.

We tend to think of radio as television without pictures, but this is not true. Radio *does* have pictures, but we create them ourselves in our mind's eye, and nothing flashes a picture up on the screen in our heads more effectively than the sound of something with which we are familiar. The best radio journalism blends actuality sound with the journalist's words. Sound is often used before we hear any words, as a means of setting the scene.

Holding the attention of the listener in the linear medium of radio is vital. An effective way of doing this is to offer the listener fresh sounds at frequent intervals. In addition to the journalist's voice and actuality sound, radio pieces can ring the changes in a number of other ways.

Interviews are essential to most sports stories, and clips of interviews with one or more of the people involved in the story not only give listeners the opportunity of hearing what they sound like, and therefore forming an opinion about them as people, but also add variety to the sounds we are hearing. VOX POPS with fans can be used in a similar way.

Another option open to the sports broadcaster is to inject interest and drama into a piece by using clips from commentaries. The excitement generated by the best commentators at climactic moments in sporting events will immediately change the tone and pace of a radio piece, and help produce more pictures in the mind.

Music, too, is part of the language of radio. Sports fans often invent and sing their own songs, which can be used to good effect by journalists. And many sports lend themselves to musical interpretation, whether through the words of a pop song or the tune or rhythms of a classical piece. Music can be used for emphasis at appropriate points, or simply used unobtrusively underneath the words to create a mood. Listeners who might otherwise lose interest in radio items have been known to stick with them just to listen to their favourite music.

Radio elements checklist

- Actuality sound
- Journalist's voice
- Interview clips
- Commentary clips
- Vox pops
- Music

Television

Television is a picture-led medium, and professional sport, which depends for its existence on spectators, is ideally suited to television. Moving pictures convey the action as it happens, but they also provide the key element in television reportage. The quality of the pictures available to a television journalist normally determines the importance attached to a story, and even whether the story is used at all. With sport, of course, getting hold of dramatic pictures to illustrate a story is rarely a problem. However, pictures provide only one element in the language of television.

Television uses many of the elements of radio journalism: actuality sound (known in television as NATSOF, natural sound on film), a journalist's voice over pictures (VOICEOVER, or v/o), interview clips, commentary clips, vox pops and music. But the language of television is even more varied and complex than that of radio. In addition to contemporaneous moving pictures, television can also use still photographs, archive material, captions and signs to help tell its stories, and because it engages two of our senses – sight and hearing – it is capable of delivering information through both at the same time. The secret of good television journalism is to use pictures, words, sound and sometimes music, together and in harmony, to squeeze as much information as possible into every moment of screen time.

While a journalist is telling us something in a voiceover, we can also be seeing action or perhaps gathering additional information from captions or signage. These additional elements can be used by journalists to provide information that otherwise would have to be included in their voiceovers. A good television script uses not only words, but also pictures and other elements in unison, as we shall see below.

Television elements checklist

- Moving pictures
- Words
- Stills
- Archive material
- NATSOF
- Interview clips
- Vox pops
- Commentary
- Captions
- Signage
- Music

Online

Because websites can offer a hybrid of print and audio and video clips, they can use a combination of all the above elements (see Chapter 10).

INSIDE RADIO AND TELEVISION SPORTS DEPARTMENTS

Radio and television companies organise their sports coverage in different ways, depending on their size and local circumstances. Sport forms an integral part of most broadcast news bulletins, and many channels employ specialist reporters to provide sports news coverage. Sometimes they will be part of a bigger sports department which also makes feature programmes and provides live event coverage – OUTSIDE BROADCASTS (or OBs).

Many companies, however, particularly in television, use independent production companies to provide feature and OB material. Because of the specialised equipment and expertise involved, it is often more cost-effective to contract such productions out to companies which specialise in sport. For the same reason, most broadcasters use freelance commentators and expert analysts.

SPORTS NEWS

The amount of airtime devoted to sports news on radio and television varies from short slots in general news bulletins or news magazine programmes to dedicated sports news channels providing continuous, rolling coverage.

Although the rights to cover most major sporting events are now sold to individual broadcasters, this does not preclude other broadcasters from providing news coverage before and after the event. Clubs and organisations are anxious to maximise their pre-event publicity to generate interest in their events and fill their stadiums. Similarly, broadcasters who own the rights to an event can expect bigger audiences if it is plugged in advance on rival channels. Pre-event press conferences and interviews with players and coaches are therefore usually open to all broadcast media, though some of them may choose not to publicise events being shown on competing channels.

After the event, reciprocal NEWS ACCESS agreements often allow television broadcasters who do not own the rights to show clips of the action on their news programmes.

The design of websites has had an important influence on the way television sports news is presented, especially on dedicated sports news channels and in 'results service' programmes. Although live presenters are still used to introduce news stories and packages, their images on screen now tend to be surrounded by text. In the manner of websites, the viewer is bombarded with continuously changing information in SIDEBARS and in CRAWLERS along the bottom of the screen, a development driven by a growing demand for sports statistics and for regular and immediate scores and results updates.

WHAT BROADCAST SPORTS JOURNALISTS DO

A successful broadcast journalist needs a wide range of skills. They include reading and writing bulletins, the presentation of programmes, interviewing, commentary, writing for websites and for social media sites, building relationships with key contacts, and researching and breaking stories. But like their print and online counterparts, the most important of these skills is writing. Broadcast journalists must be able to work across the whole range of journalistic platforms. They will be expected to write for radio, television and websites, breaking and updating stories, as well as synthesising those stories into 140-character blocks for social media sites. They must build sound relationships with sports professionals and the chief executives and press officers of sports organisations. A broadcast journalist's work depends on being able to conduct face-to-face interviews, and the ability to do this will often be based on trust. When times are bad – after a defeat, for instance – many coaches will only give interviews, or provide honest answers, to journalists they know and trust. And because broadcast journalists have to be where the action is, the ability to drive is essential.

A DAY IN THE LIFE OF A BROADCAST SPORTS JOURNALIST

The first thing all journalists need to do when they arrive at work is to catch up with what has been happening while they have been away. For a sports journalist that means checking the websites of the clubs and organisations in their areas, whether it be at local or national level, and the site of the organisation for whom you are working and its major competitors, as well as the sports sites of the major organisations such as the BBC and Sky. Checking on what your rivals are doing has become more important than ever in the social media age. Most sports journalists are active on these sites. They will break stories there as soon as they have them and before they start to write for their own organisations. Their rivals will retweet and analyse those stories, and credit and develop other people's stories under their own hashtags. Social media has now turned sports journalism into a communal job, in which one of your most important sources is other journalists.

Multiplatform working has made life a lot busier for broadcast sports journalists, whose workloads have increased accordingly. Many now have to provide their material for radio, online, television, Facebook and Twitter. Bigger organisations may have online teams to process stories for the web, which can be a specialised task demanding a close knowledge of particular software, but they still rely on 'frontline' journalists to provide them with their information and audio or video material.

But the main focus remains regular contributions to the sports segments of news bulletins, which on radio can be as frequent as every hour, with longer slots at lunch and drivetime. And in the evenings there may be phone-in programmes to fill. All this requires a regular flow of stories, many of which will be developed from news agency SNAPS which flow into the office throughout the day. On days when there is a busy sports programme, early bulletins may contain recorded preview chats with a presenter to tease audiences into tuning in to the station's later coverage of events. On busy shows a reporter may have the help of a producer, who will select and cut (edit) recorded inserts and act as a second pair of eyes. And then, of course, there are the live reports or commentaries from events, which we will discuss in detail later in this chapter.

STORY STRUCTURE

But the bread and butter of broadcast sports journalists is the stories with which daily bulletins are filled. These usually follow a number of standard formats, which are similar in radio and television. The format in which a broadcast news story is presented will vary according to the importance of the story, the time available to produce it and the elements with which the journalist has to work.

Television

News stories in television tend to fall into one of four categories (Table 9.1, p. 121). The terms used to refer to them may vary from country to country, and even between media organisations in the same country, but they can be summarised as follows:

Camera read

The simplest television news story is known as a CAMERA READ. The bulletin presenter, who is in vision throughout, simply reads copy from a script visible on the AUTOCUE. Camera reads are written to get breaking stories on air quickly, or when no pictures are available to accompany the story.

Example

Bulletin reader: We've just heard that the former Brazil soccer captain Socrates has died at the age of 57. Socrates played in two World Cups, won 60 caps for his country between 1979 and 1986 and scored 22 goals.

Underlay - sometimes known as an OOV (out of vision)

If pictures are available, shot specifically for the purpose or taken from the library of recorded material that all television stations keep, they can be screened to illustrate the story the presenter is reading. This type of story is called an UNDERLAY. The presenter remains in vision while reading the LINK to the story. Pictures are then run under the presenter's voice as the story continues. The pictures which are available will dictate the way the story is written.

Example

Link: The former Brazil soccer captain Socrates has died at the age of 57.

  V/o (bulletin reader's voice over pictures)

  It was goals like this that earned Socrates the reputation of one of the greatest midfielders to play the game. He scored 172 goals in 297 games for Brazilian club side Corinthians after starting his career with Botafogo. He spent one season at Fiorentina, in Italy.

Upsound - sometimes known as an SOT (sound on tape)

If an interview or interviews are available, clips from them can be run on the end of an underlay, turning it into an UPSOUND. What the interviewees say in their clips will influence the way the preceding script is written. Note how the link has now moved the story on from the fact of Socrates' death to the tributes that are starting to flow in. It is important to start with the latest angle in a running story like this.

Example

Link: The world of football has been paying tribute to Socrates, the former Brazil captain, who has died at the age of 57.

V/o

The midfielder, who scored 22 goals for his country and who also had a degree in medicine, had been critically ill in intensive care in hospital in Sao Paulo with an intestinal infection. He died as his former club, Corinthians, won their first Brazilian League title for six years. Fans held up signs honouring Socrates, and players stood in silence before the final game.

Interview clip (Corinthians striker Liedson)

'The Corinthians nation woke up very sad today because of the loss of this incredible person. The title comes as a small way to honour him.'

Package

An important or complex story will usually be presented as a PACKAGE. This involves a reporter bringing together on tape a number of elements, usually including voiceovers and interview clips. Packages may also include vox pops, a PIECE TO CAMERA by the reporter, archive material, still pictures, NATSOF and music. The bulletin presenter reads a link to introduce the pre-recorded tape which has been compiled by another journalist. Each of the elements is kept short – usually a maximum of 20 seconds – to hold the viewer's attention. Note how this package reuses some of the material used earlier, but incorporates it into a longer and much more varied piece which makes full use of the various elements that make up the language of television.

Example

Link: Socrates, one of the greatest soccer players of his age, has died. Brazil's captain in two World Cups had been in a critical condition in hospital with an intestinal infection. This report from Jim Smith.

Package (Jim Smith's voice over today's pictures of players and fans observing a minute's silence)

(Continued)

(Continued)

A silent tribute to a legend of the game. Players and fans show their respect for a footballing giant ahead of the Corinthians versus Palmeiras match, in which his former club secured the Brazilian League title for the first time in six years.

Interview clip (Corinthians striker Liedson)

'The Corinthians nation woke up very sad today because of the loss of this incredible person. The title comes as a small way to honour him.'

V/o (archive footage of Socrates during his playing career)

Socrates won 60 caps for his country and scored 22 goals. He was known for his physical strength. Six feet four inches tall, he was also a two-footed player of great vision and skill, and it was goals like this that brought him to the attention of the entire football world.

Vox pops (short clips of fans)

'He was the greatest player I ever saw in a Brazil shirt.'

'He was a footballing genius, a talented and sophisticated player.'

'He had everything – he was a great midfielder and a qualified doctor.'

V/o (archive shots of Socrates playing for Fiorentina and Garforth Town)

Though he played most of his football in Brazil, he also spent one season with Fiorentina in Italy. At the age of 50 he came out of retirement to make a one-off appearance as player-coach for the English non-league club Garforth Town. He played just 12 minutes as a substitute.

Interview clip (Zico, former Brazil team-mate)

'He was a spectacular guy. He was one of the best I ever played with. His intelligence was unique.'

V/o (library footage of Socrates working as a pundit on Brazilian TV)

In retirement, Socrates worked as a doctor, dabbled in politics and made a reputation as a journalist and sports pundit on Brazilian television.

(Recent still photograph)

He was also a heavy smoker and admitted to problems with alcohol.

Socrates died today.

Discussion

Notice how the package moves quickly from element to element and from action shots to talking heads, to maintain the interest of the viewer. Mixing packages with upsounds and underlays within a bulletin also helps to maintain the viewer's interest.

EXERCISE

Write a television package about 90 seconds long using the following newspaper story as your source. Scripts are normally read at about three words a second, but using all the elements of television language available to you will help you cram a lot of information into a minute and a half.

Assume you can film whatever you wish, and interview whoever you wish. Set out your script in the same way as the one above, indicating where each element begins, and describing the pictures which will accompany the voiceovers. You should try to make an impact with your opening shots (or sounds, if you are writing a radio script) to grab the audience's attention.

First, write a link to introduce the story. Write the script for your package, including the wording of any interview clips and vox pops you are using. List the pictures you intend to use in brackets above the text they will illustrate. This will help you see how the elements you intend to use will fit together. You should use captions to give the names and positions of interviewees. This means you will not have to name them in your voiceovers. Similarly, locations can be identified by shots of signs or buildings.

News story

China's Olympic team will fly into London tomorrow on a mission to confirm their position as the world's leading Olympic nation.

Four years ago in Beijing, they finished top of the medals table for the first time to announce to the world that China had become a sporting, as well as an economic, superpower.

Their 51 gold medals were the result of a £3 billion national training programme that identifies potential talent as young as five and provides a demanding coaching regime which has become a production line for sporting champions.

Starting with disciplines like table tennis, volleyball and badminton, which need few resources, the country's sports administrators are now setting their sights on more sophisticated events like tennis, in which Li Na became their first Grand Slam winner when she lifted the French Open title.

China will be represented in 23 sports in London, where Sun Yang is expected to become their first male champion in the pool.

And after decades of cultural isolation, China wants to use the London Olympics to further the country's integration into the international community.

(Continued)

117

(Continued)

> The table tennis squad, which won all 24 available medals in Beijing, have been given English lessons before leaving for London so that they can speak for their country outside the Olympic venues, as well as in them.

Suggested answer

Link: China's Olympic team will fly into London tomorrow on a mission to confirm their position as the world's leading Olympic nation. Jane Jones reports from Beijing.

Package script

(Chinese music beneath entire package)

(Opening shot of volleyball squad training in the open air. NATSOF of players' voices. Camera pulls back to reveal skyscrapers on modern Beijing skyline.)

V/o: Training hard for the London Games – China's athletes are determined to show the world this country is now a sporting, as well as an economic, superpower. They gave notice of that when the Olympics were held here in Beijing four years ago.

NATSOF (original commentary over archive pictures of China winning gold medals in Beijing) And that's another table tennis medal for China... China win gold again... Another gold for the host nation...

V/o: We already know China as an industrial power *(shots of metal being poured in steelworks)* but it's in camps like this that the country's sporting future is being forged. *(Shots of children practising gymnastics)* Children as young as five are already being trained to become the champions of the future.

(Interview clip with training camp manager)

V/o: Many in the West still think of China as a closed community *(shots of the walls of Beijing's Forbidden City)* but now they are using sport to reach out to the rest of the world. *(Shots of table tennis squad in classroom learning English)*

NATSOF (squad speaking English)

V/o: Compulsory English lessons for their all-conquering table tennis team so that they can speak on behalf of China to the rest of the world in London.

(Interview clip with table tennis player)

V/o: They won 51 golds and finished top of the medals table at the Beijing Games. *(Shots of medal ceremony with Chinese flag and anthem)* And now, with the hopes of the world's most populous nation riding on them *(shots of athletes boarding coach for airport)*, they are determined to show they can do it again – this time, outside China. *(Shots of crowd around coach waving Chinese flags)*

Fade up Chinese music.

Discussion

The television package uses many of the resources of the language of the medium. Notice how the link is almost identical to the newspaper intro. The reporter's name-check stresses that she is reporting from China, which adds authority to the piece.

The Chinese music sets the scene and holds the package together, while the script is shaped by the pictures the reporter uses. Starting with shots of players in training takes us straight to the heart of the story. The voiceover puts the pictures into context, and pulling back to a wide shot of the modern skyscrapers cleverly reflects the words of the reporter's script.

The second sentence then provides a smooth transition to archive footage of the Beijing Games, and the quick cuts from sport to sport and use of the original commentary injects an element of excitement into the package. By cutting from NATSOF to voiceover to commentary to voiceover and now to interview clip, we maintain the viewers' interest by never letting them get bored with listening to the same voice for too long. The choice of interviewee follows logically from the pictures we have just been watching.

In the second v/o, the shots of molten metal being poured and children doing gymnastics have again been chosen for their visual impact, and graphically illustrate the reporter's words. Similarly, the next voiceover is an excuse to use some tourist shots of Beijing's Forbidden City (again, to maintain interest). The script connects them logically to the next sequence, in the language lab, which provides us with more NATSOF, this time in English. The next interview clip, with a player, is also in English. When covering stories involving sports people whose first language is not your own, try to find interviewees who can speak your language. This will make their clips seem more direct, although you should be prepared to translate their words into your language, and use captions or get someone else to read the translation.

The final voiceover fills in some of the background statistics to the story, with more colourful archive footage. This has been chosen to give the final sequence a flags theme. We see flags again in the crowd which has assembled to see the athletes off to London, bringing the story right up to date.

Because almost all professional sports events are now filmed, archive material is one of the most useful tools for television sports journalists. It is almost always possible to find shots of the people or events they require. These should, however, be interspersed with newly shot material where possible. In this piece, shots of the Beijing skyline and the Forbidden City provide local flavour and added interest for the viewer, and the voiceover subtly weaves them into the Olympic narrative. Thus the package has used many of the elements of television language to convey a lot of information in a short space of time.

Radio

Radio bulletins are also made up of a similar mix of stories which are roughly equivalent to those in television (Table 9.1, p. 121). The simplest is a COPY ITEM read by the newsreader – the equivalent of a camera read on television. If more information is available, a reporter may be asked to write a VOICEPIECE, a free-standing story introduced by the bulletin presenter by means of a CUE, which is the radio equivalent of a link. If interview clips are available, these can be attached to the end of a copy item or voicepiece – to produce the radio equivalent of an upsound. Sometimes an interview clip will be dropped into the middle of a voicepiece.

As in television, an important or complex story will be presented as a package if the required elements are available. Radio packages closely follow the style of their television equivalents (see above). They will normally include the reporter's voice and interview clips, and may also include vox pops, clips of match commentary, archive material, actuality sound and music.

EXERCISE

Compile a radio package on the Olympics story dealt with above, identifying any actuality sound or other elements you will use.

OTHER OPTIONS

Both radio and television have other options available to them for varying and extending their sports news coverage. Packages are often used as the basis for a studio discussion, with guests invited in to comment on the subject of the story.

Packages can be given greater immediacy with a LIVE or AS-LIVE introduction by a reporter at the scene. Standing a reporter outside a stadium gives the impression that he or she is on the spot to cover the story as it is unfolding. When reporters introduce and end ('top and tail') their pieces in this way, the packages are known as DOUGHNUTS, because the package fills the hole in the middle.

If a story is just breaking and no package is available, the same effect can be achieved by doing a TWO-WAY INTERVIEW with the reporter at the scene or by getting the reporter to do a live interview there with an expert who can comment on the story.

If no means of sending live pictures from a location is available, the same effect can be achieved by recording a piece as if it were live and sending the tape back to the studios. Such pieces are known as 'as-lives'.

WRITING AND PERFORMING SCRIPTS

In broadcasting, it is not enough to produce sharp, informative, entertaining scripts, although all these things are important. Scripts must be written in a way that makes them easy to read. This will often mean writing short, simple sentences with no sub-clauses.

Broadcasting is a performance and the way in which a journalist reads a script on air influences the audience's perception of the story. Scripts should be read with

Table 9.1 Types of story

Radio	TV
Copy item – read by bulletin reader	Camera read
Voicepiece – read by reporter	Underlay
Copy item or voicepiece with clip	Upsound
Package – mix of reporter and clips	Package
Studio guest/interview – often off back of package	
Lives/as-lives	
Cue (same as a newspaper intro)	Link

confidence and authority (and occasionally with wit or charm or solemnity). This is easier to do if you are performing your own material, because you can write it in a way you will find easy to read. Most of us find some words or phrases difficult to pronounce. It is a good idea to read each sentence out loud after you have written it to make sure you can get your tongue round it easily and smoothly. Read the whole script out loud when you have finished it and before you attempt to record it. Change it, if necessary, to make it more comfortable to read – such as rephrasing a sentence or choosing an alternative word. And always rehearse your performance before recording the script or reading it live.

Scripts should be performed in a way that enhances their meaning for the listener. This means that the more important words should be emphasised (see below). Try to avoid a monotonous and unvaried delivery or you will lose the listener's attention. It is often a good idea to emphasise the first word, as this grabs the listener's attention.

Don't be afraid to change a script written by someone else (providing you don't alter the sense of it) if you are uncomfortable with it, as no two people have the same reading style. Bulletin readers always read through the whole bulletin before they go on air, and change any words or sentences with which they feel uncomfortable.

EXERCISE

Go through the package you have written and underline the key words you need to emphasise when you record it. Aim to vary the pitch and tone of your voice, hitting the emphasised words harder.

Now perform your script and get colleagues to offer constructive criticism, or record it and criticise yourself. Repeat the exercise and see whether you can improve your delivery. If you are unhappy with your first attempt to record a script, do it again – and again, if necessary. Always listen carefully to the way professional journalists deliver their scripts and try to learn from them.

PERFORMING IN VISION

Television journalists sometimes perform in vision as well as recording voiceovers for their packages. If you are doing a piece to camera, try to make that interesting too. Watching a reporter walk through an appropriate location – the pits at a motor racing track, for instance, or among the weights and exercise bikes in a gym – is much more interesting and informative than seeing the journalist standing still in the same location. The changing background gives the viewer a much better feel for the atmosphere. Even more effective is to demonstrate to the camera what you are talking about: deliver part of your report while skiing down a section of the slalom course, or from behind the wheel of a Formula 1 or rally car.

BROADCAST INTERVIEWS

The interview is an important ingredient of almost any form of broadcast sports journalism. It is a vital element in upsounds and packages, and in the build-up to or aftermath of live or recorded-highlights coverage of events. Many of the guidelines for newspaper interviews (see Chapter 5) apply equally to broadcast interviews. However, it is fairly easy for a print journalist to select random sentences or even phrases from the dullest interview and produce an interesting piece. For a broadcast interview to be effective, on the other hand, it is crucial that the interviewee should sound and look interesting. It is important, therefore, for the interviewer to coax an interesting performance out of the interviewee, especially if the interview is live and there is no scope for editing.

Setting up an interview

It can be easier to persuade sports personalities to give one-to-one interviews to radio or television than to the print media. They know that what they say cannot be distorted (although it can be used selectively). Appearing on radio or television appeals to the egos of many people, and those who have been involved in sport at a senior level will be used to the broadcast media. They are unlikely to be nervous of microphones or television cameras.

Against that must be set the additional demands broadcasters frequently impose on them. It is often necessary to persuade interviewees to come into a studio or to go to a specific location which will provide a suitable backdrop for the interview. In such cases, journalists should always be prepared to provide taxis or other forms of transport if necessary, and to make sure they do not waste the time of their interviewees by keeping them waiting.

Interview technique

Choosing the location for an interview should be the first consideration. A suitable background (or appropriate background sounds) help to set the mood. On radio, the sound of bookmakers shouting the odds will transport the listener to the racetrack. On television, interviewing an ice hockey coach on the rink or a rower in front of the boat shed has the same effect. Similarly, what the interviewee is wearing (a track suit or team shirt) helps to provide the right context. Television interviews can also make use of an ESTABLISHING SHOT – a shot of the interviewee, preferably involved in the sport he or she represents, shown immediately before a clip of the interview, to establish the person's identity in the viewers' minds

The importance of sponsorship in sport means that some interviewees will insist on doing interviews in front of boards which contain the names and logos of their sponsors. Many broadcasters now accept this as inevitable, but overt advertising conflicts with the guidelines of some broadcast organisations. It may be necessary to ask an interviewee to remove a cap or other item of clothing which displays commercial branding, or to get the camera operator to frame the shot so that it is not visible.

No matter how experienced your interviewee (and many managers and coaches do dozens of radio and television interviews every week), it is important to put them at ease before the interview begins. A joke off-camera or before the recorder is switched on will break the ice, relax the interviewee and establish a comfortable relationship with the interviewer. This is particularly important if the prime aim of the interview is to bring out the personality of the interviewee.

Most radio interviews are one to one, but television interviews may involve several people (a journalist, a camera operator, a sound recordist and sometimes a director or producer). This can make some interviewees nervous, although this is less frequently a problem than it once was. Television crews have reduced in size in recent years. It is now usual to have just a reporter and a camera operator, or even a one-person crew – a video-journalist, or VJ. If an interviewee is intimidated by the size of the crew, the numbers can be reduced by letting the journalist handle the microphone.

Another method of relaxing television interviewees is to try to get them to ignore the camera. In any event, interviewees should never stare into the camera. Instead, they should look slightly off-camera, at the interviewer. This gives viewers the impression that they are eavesdropping on a conversation. The easiest way of achieving this is to tell the interviewee: 'Ignore the camera and just talk to me.'

Most broadcast interviews are pre-recorded, and in many cases the journalist will be interested only in a brief SOUNDBITE for use as part of a package. In such cases it is important to try to get the most appropriate form of words, expressed in a lively or concise way.

The interviewer should listen carefully to the way answers are phrased. If they are not lively enough, or contain too many ums and ers, or the language used is too complex, the interviewer should try to find a different way of asking the question, perhaps at a later stage in the interview, when the interviewee has relaxed a little. This will often produce a different and perhaps more usable version of the answer. In the last resort, perhaps if the person has made two related points in different answers which will be difficult to edit together, he or she could be asked to repeat them in a single sentence. But interviewers should always avoid putting words in people's mouths.

Some people can be animated and articulate and even difficult to shut up before the camera or recorder is switched on, and then give one-word or single-sentence answers when the interview begins. It is sometimes helpful to tell people in advance what you are going to ask them, and explain the purpose of the interview to them. Indeed, you should always do so if they ask. Interviews are not intended to catch people out but to help them express their views clearly. However, it rarely pays to rehearse a broadcast interview or spend a long time chatting informally about the subject matter before you begin. This tends to make interviewees feel they have already answered your questions, and so they are rarely as open or forthcoming in the real interview.

Always try to use OPEN QUESTIONS, which cannot be answered by a simple yes or no. Try to avoid anticipating the interviewee's likely views in your question (*You must be delighted with the result?*) because this invites them merely to agree with you.

It is important that the interviewer should sound confident and well-informed. It is a good idea to prepare questions in advance. You will not have time (especially if your interview is live) to try to remember questions you have forgotten, so write them down if necessary.

It is a good idea to start with a general question (*What's your view of the game?*) and ask specific questions as follow-ups if they have not already been covered in an earlier answer. If you are not to lose the attention of your audience, you should not allow answers to continue for too long – 20 or 30 seconds is often enough. Don't interrupt too often, but be prepared to do so if the answers to your questions are too expansive, stray from the subject or are just plain boring.

If an interview is live, you will be working to a strict time limit. Tell your interviewee in advance how long the interview will last, and agree on a pre-arranged signal you will use when you want it to end. Try to shape the interview so that you cover all the points you want to within the time available.

EXERCISE

Get a fellow student or colleague to read reports of a game or event and play the role of a competitor or coach in an interview. Prepare your questions and record your interview, on camera if possible. Play it back and listen to or watch it critically. If you do not have access to recording equipment, conduct a series of interviews as a group. Listen to and watch the interviews of your colleagues and offer constructive feedback.

You should always watch or listen critically to the interviews conducted by professional journalists on radio or television, and try to learn from them. With packages, listen to the interview clips that have been used and ask yourself how they have helped the reporter to tell the story.

COVERING EVENTS

The big advantage broadcasters (especially television broadcasters) have over the print media is that they can take their audiences direct to events. They can cover sporting action live, or broadcast it after the event, in its entirety or as HIGHLIGHTS. But their access to events will normally depend on whether they have bought the rights from the people (normally a sports governing body, but sometimes individual clubs or promoters) who own them.

Rights

The rights to a sporting event will normally be sold to the highest bidder, although a broadcasting organisation which can offer more exposure for the sport, or a higher standard of coverage, may be preferred. Individual events will often be included in a wider package which will give the same broadcaster access to all the games in a particular league or cup competition, or series, for instance, or all the races at a particular track. Rights are normally sold for periods of several years, which makes it cost-effective for broadcasters to establish the expensive infrastructure required to cover sports events live.

Sports often maximise their rights income by selling rights in a number of countries (although pictures will normally be provided by a single broadcaster), secondary rights to show highlights packages, pay-per-view games and radio rights.

Live broadcasts

Because broadcasters pay a lot of money for sporting rights, they want to get as much value from them as possible. Live events (usually known as outside broadcasts or OBs) are now typically broadcast as part of an extended package which sandwiches the action between pre- and post-match slots. To brand their programmes and give a taste of the excitement to come, broadcasters often spend a lot of money on an opening graphics sequence before the presenter introduces the programme. The build-up to the event typically involves pre-match interviews with players and coaches, discussion between expert guests (often current or former players or coaches) and features or news packages on the players or teams involved. The event itself may be followed by post-match interviews, expert analysis and a highlights package of other games in the same competition. It will often end with a sequence of the key incidents set to music. Again, the priority is to vary the content to maintain the interest of the audience.

Broadcast coverage, therefore, follows a similar pattern to that of print journalism discussed in Chapter 6 – build-up, preview, event coverage, inquest – but condensed into a much narrower time-frame, which will often be a single programme.

An outside broadcast of a sporting event is a complex technical and logistical operation which requires a great deal of planning, the mobilisation of expensive equipment and contributions from professionals in a wide range of disciplines. For that reason they are often carried out by specialist companies contracted to the broadcasters who own the principal rights to the event. Because televised sport is now a global industry, the company covering the event may also be providing a 'feed' of its pictures to a number of other domestic and foreign broadcasters, who will arrange their own commentary and analysis.

OUTSIDE BROADCASTS

Radio outside broadcasts are relatively simple affairs, often involving a single journalist, perhaps accompanied by a summariser and a technician, using a permanent line linked to the studio. A live television outside broadcast, on the other hand, is a major technical and logistical operation. The biggest sporting events, such as the Olympic Games, can involve hundreds of cameras and journalists working from dozens of different locations over a period of several weeks. But even one-off events involve large numbers of people and a great deal of sophisticated equipment.

The exact set-up for a live outside broadcast will depend on the nature of the sport being covered, but the approach is usually similar. The following sections describe how a live soccer match might be covered.

Cameras

The principal coverage will be provided by two fixed cameras placed on the television gantry, which is usually suspended from the roof of the main stand of the stadium, level with the half-way line. One camera provides wide shots of the playing area; the other provides close-ups.

There will be additional cameras at the side of the pitch, to provide tight close-ups of the players, the coaches and substitutes on the bench, and of the crowd. These are useful for goal celebrations, when players are being treated for injuries, and for shots of the reactions of the crowd and coaches to key incidents. At least one will be a roaming camera, known as a STEADICAM. These are attached to their operators by a frame, which allows them to move up and down the touchline to get closer to an incident.

There will be a camera behind and slightly to the side of each goal, to record goals and goalmouth incidents, and to provide replays from a different angle from the gantry cameras. There may also be cameras midway between goals and half-way line, principally to cover offside decisions. There may also be a camera on a crane, a wire suspended across the half-way line, or even attached to a balloon suspended above the stadium, to provide aerial shots.

All the cameras are situated on the same side of the pitch, to avoid confusing viewers about the direction in which teams are playing. The camera operators follow instructions issued by the director. They can also hear the match commentary.

Commentators and analysts

The commentary team will normally have a high vantage point on the half-way line. They, too, are in contact with the director. The presenter and analysts providing pre- and post-match comment will normally be in a separate studio or box.

Director and technicians

The pictures are controlled from a scanner truck which is normally parked outside the stadium. Inside are a series of television monitors which show the pictures being shot by each camera. The director selects which of these to screen at any given moment, and asks camera operators to get specific shots. Sports coverage normally consists of a mix of wide, medium and close shots, intercut quite quickly. It is the responsibility of the director to make sure this is done smoothly and unobtrusively, and that shots of key moments, preferably from more than one angle, are always available. The director will also be in touch with the commentary team and will give advance warning that certain shots will be used – such as a celebrity in the crowd – so that appropriate reference can be made in commentary.

All the pictures are recorded on a series of machines controlled by a replay technician whose job is to provide instant action replays when requested to do so by the director. The crew will also include a sound engineer and other technicians.

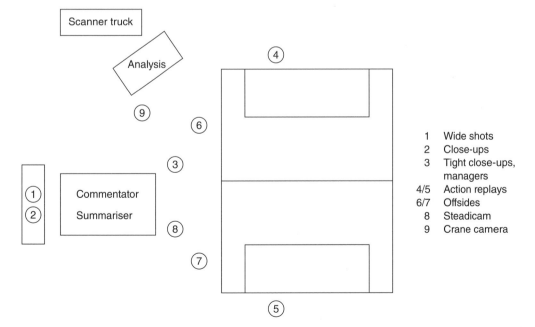

Figure 9.1 Set-up for major outside broadcast

Events being covered specifically for inclusion in highlights packages will normally be taped by a single camera operator, usually working from a gantry high above the arena, which gives a good, uninterrupted view of the action. The operator will switch between wide shots, medium shots and close-ups, as the action dictates.

Because highlights sequences often have to be edited quickly, it is essential that the camera operator keeps an accurate LOG of the key moments in the action. Television tapes are time-coded in hours, minutes and seconds, and the log gives the times at which goals, near-misses, injuries, interesting close-ups and EDIT POINTS (e.g. shots of crowd reaction used as cutaways) occur. This allows editors who have the task of reducing, say, a 90-minute soccer match to two minutes of airtime, to quickly find the sequences they need from the RUSHES – the unedited tapes.

Example: Tape log

Dayton v Exfield

00.08.20 Dayton hit post
00.11.40 Exfield good chance
00.17.00 Robins goal 1-0
00.22.10 Exfield shot over
00.34.50 Dayton header wide
00.42.10 Jameson goal 1-1
00.47.50 Exfield free kick and shot saved
00.56.00 Dayton good shot saved
01.01.30 Dayton cross and chance missed
01.07.10 Smith goal 1-2
01.10.20 Exfield penalty claim
01.19.10 Dayton run and shot saved
01.26.20 Jones goal 2-2

COMMENTARY

The skills of which viewers and listeners are most aware when sport is being broadcast are those of the journalists, commentators and expert summarisers who describe and explain the action. They require the same in-depth knowledge of their sports as their colleagues in print journalism, but their skills and working practices are often different.

Most print journalists covering a sporting event work on their own, but broadcast journalists almost always work as part of a team. This may include fellow commentators and summarisers as well as a director and technicians. For long events such as cricket and tennis matches, they may work in shifts of 15 minutes or so, sharing commentary with half a dozen others. It is essential to establish a good working relationship with other members of the team.

Although sports broadcasters are often regarded as having glamorous jobs, their work often involves travelling long distances, working long hours, arriving at an event early and leaving late. And if the job is to be done well, it involves hours of painstaking preparation.

Research and preparation

Broadcasters who are covering events live must have all the information they require at their fingertips – inside their heads or in easily accessible note form. Live commentary demands instant reaction, and this means doing your homework.

Commentators will usually be told which event they are covering well in advance. If it is to take place on a Saturday, they will begin their preparation and research on Thursday. This may involve carrying out pre-event recorded interviews, and will certainly mean looking at the websites of the clubs involved and at preview coverage in other media. It is vital that you are aware of recent results and stories involving the participants, so read what everybody else has to say, look at the local newspapers, research the statistics. Was there anything remarkable about the previous meetings involving the participants? When did the visitors last win at this venue? Look at the five previous fixtures of each team, and be aware of who they will come up against in their next five.

This is information you will need for your own preview, and some of it will be useful during commentary. So get it all written down. You may never look at these notes, but it will stick in your mind, ready for retrieval when you need it. You must also do some research on each of the players who will be taking part, including substitutes. Make notes on their ages, performance histories, how many yellow or red cards they currently have against their names, how many goals or runs they have scored this season, how many appearances they have made, their disciplinary records, international appearances, other teams they have played for, and so on. Try also to find out two bits of other information about each player – hobbies, tastes in clothes or music. If a performer does something of note, it may be necessary to talk about them at some length, so background information about each of them is essential.

Commentators must also have the information necessary to put the event into context. They must be aware of the significance of the result for both teams, the results of any previous games between them, the sequences of victories or defeats, the consequences for coaches or managers of victory or defeat. And look back at recent team formations so that you can make an educated guess during your preview remarks about what they are likely to look like for this fixture.

Working suggestion: *None of this will be much good unless it is easily accessible during commentary. One useful tip is to write the details about each player on a separate* *sticker, and attach them to a piece of A5 card, in team formation, one team on each side of the card. You can hold the card in your hand at all times for instant reference during commentary, turning it over when necessary, without taking your eyes off the field of play. When players leave the field, take their stickers off the card and replace them with the substitutes' stickers. Tape other statistics and information to the desk for easy reference.*

It is essential for commentators to recognise the players and competitors taking part in the event. Many now wear their numbers and names on their shirts, of course, but it is not always possible to see them in the thick of the action. In some sports they don't have them, so commentators must be able to identify people by sight. If unfamiliar performers are involved, study videos or team photographs before the event, but even faces can be indistinct at the opposite end of a sports field. Many commentators try to find ways of identifying people at a glance – the player wearing white boots; the one with his or her shirt outside their shorts; the fat, bald one or the tall, thin one.

EXERCISE

Choose a sporting event which is to be televised and prepare to do a commentary on it. You will need to recognise the competitors who are expected to take part and to make notes on them. You will also need to research the information you will need to put the event in context. Use some of the sources outlined in Chapter 4. When you have made your notes, read them through and try to memorise as much of the information as possible.

On air

Commentary teams are typically made up of professional journalists, whose basic skills are with words, and SUMMARISERS, who are often former players or coaches, chosen for their knowledge of the sport and tactics. The journalists, however, also need to have expert knowledge of the sports they are covering, and the summarisers should be articulate: not all former sports people are.

Covering a sporting event live is different from most other forms of broadcast journalism. It consists largely of unscripted talk. Audiences who are used to listening to carefully scripted material will expect the same high standards. Waffle will not do.

Although the action itself will often be strong enough to hold the interest of the audience, regular changes of voice within the commentary team also stop audiences becoming bored. The best commentaries often feel as if the listener is eavesdropping on a conversation between two keen and knowledgeable fans. But radio and television commentary pose different challenges.

Radio commentary

On the day

When you go to an event, be sure to dress appropriately. You are representing your organisation at all times. You may also be quite well known. Fans may come up to you in the car park. Give them a little time and treat them courteously. Anything less could quickly give you a bad name on Twitter.

Get to the venue early. Radio commentators are usually required to set up and check the reliability of their own broadcasting equipment. Most like to arrive no less than two hours before the start of the event. This is especially important if they are expected to contribute to the build-up, which could be on air an hour before the action itself begins. This allows time to set up kit and make sure the line to the studio works. Journalists are not expected to be technical experts, but they need to have an idea of basic trouble-shooting – how to change a lead, fit new batteries or check headphones. Much of this will come with experience, but sometimes it can be necessary to call technical staff or get advice down line from base. All this takes time.

Once you are confident the kit will not let you down, you can relax a little. Check where the lavatories are, get a coffee, then see what extra information you may be able to pick up that will be useful to you when your work begins. Go to the tunnel area or locker rooms, talk to the clubs' support staff, try to get a steer on the line-ups before the teamsheets are officially released. Find out which players will be on the bench or talk to local journalists to get the latest gossip around the teams.

You may need to write a preview 15 minutes before your programme is due on air, which will include the team news and a couple of sentences to set the scene for the action. These are usually no longer than 30 seconds, so again tight writing is important. Make sure you know how the studio wants you to end pieces like this and your half-time and full-time summary. This is important because the studio needs to know when you have finished so that the presenter can come straight back on air. Your OUT-WORDS will usually be something as simple as the name of the ground (Bill Bloggs at Elland Road) or scoreline (Leeds United 2, Cardiff City 0). And make sure you have a notebook handy in which to note the goals and goal times, sendings-off, bookings, chances and other key incidents. You will need these for your summaries. Don't try to rely on your memory.

Unless the event you are covering is fairly short, such as a race, the commentator will probably be working with a SUMMARISER. This will usually be a retired professional sports person, manager or coach, often associated with one of the teams taking part. The summariser's job is to provide another voice, a contrast to that of the commentator, and to provide expert opinion and add colour to the coverage. This is why summarisers are known as colour analysts in the United States. Many commentators will work with the same summariser frequently, and will have established a good working

> My job as a commentator is to draw a picture. The summariser's job is to colour it in.
>
> **Seth Bennett, sports journalist, BBC Radio 5 Live**

relationship. But it is important that commentator and summariser establish a set of ground rules before the action begins. The commentator will be describing the action and at key moments – when the ball is in the final third of the pitch at a soccer match, for example – must feel free to cut across the summariser, who must give way. Pre-arranged signals, such as a touch on the arm or a hand gesture, will be enough if the duo have a good relationship. The reason for this is that description of key moments such as goals will be used again in highlights packages and it is important that the summariser does not spoil the commentator's description by talking over him or her. Once the key incident has been described, the summariser can be brought in to explain what happened, and its significance.

The action begins

Commentary will normally begin just before the teams or athletes come out into the stadium. There may be certain ground rules to be observed throughout the commentary. Your station's policy may be to give a score check every 90 seconds and a station check every four minutes, because listeners will be tuning in all the time. You may also be expected to plug forthcoming programmes during commentary. Try to vary the way in which you deliver regular information such as this – *it's nil-nil here*; *this game is still scoreless*; *there's no score yet in this game*.

The commentator should start by setting the scene, using the information and statistics which have been so carefully researched. The summariser should be introduced, and you should run through both teams at kick-off. It is important to build up a picture of the teams and substitutes early in the event, so spend the first 10 minutes of your commentary getting your audience used to who is who. Provide them with the first names and field positions of the players (later in the game, you needn't bother with these details); outline the formations the teams are playing in and what their tactics are. Concentrate on which team has the ball, what they are doing with it, where on the field we are – midway in their own half, in the right back position, near the corner flag. Radio has no pictures, so visual description is important. It is the commentator's job to aid people's imaginations. Use descriptive words and phrases, and vary the way in which you describe things – you can *pass*, *stroke* or *slide* the ball. Use words that paint a picture – She *tiptoes with the ball* or he *dances round the defender*.

Don't, however, assume that all your listeners are male sports fans and that all they are interested in is the action. Your audience may contain a large proportion of women, who may not be especially interested in sport, but whose menfolk are at the game, and who want to keep in touch and have some idea what mood the rest of family will be in when they arrive home. Male listeners tend to want details of play, but women respond more to descriptive commentary – what colour are the shirts, what kind of boots is a player wearing, what's the weather like? – so throw some of that into your mix as well, especially during dull periods.

> " There has to be a note in your voice that says: listen to me. You need a gear to go up to at such moments. They hear the change in tone. Now they are with you!
>
> **Seth Bennett** "

Slack moments can be difficult for a commentator, and this is where your earlier research pays dividends. Talk about the current stories surrounding the clubs, recap the scores elsewhere in the country, especially those which affect your game, and bring in your summariser. What interesting or funny stories can you coax out of them? Never forget that sports commentary is primarily entertainment, and no matter how good or bad the action, journalists have to entertain. A sprinkling of entertaining chat is more important than describing every kick. And don't forget that commentary is no longer simply about journalists talking to audiences. It is now a three-way conversation between commentator, summariser and listeners, who can contribute via texts and tweets. Ask for your audience's contributions, and read them out on air during slack moments. And don't be afraid to offer your own opinions. You are an expert and your opinion is as valid as anyone else's, so offer an opinion if you have something to add, if you know a lot about the subject.

It is also important to vary the tone of your delivery. Bad commentators describe everything at the same inflated level of excitement. Save that for the *really* exciting moments. Most listeners will not be hanging on your every word. They will be doing other things as well – driving, ironing, painting the shed. You are background noise. They need alerting to the key moments.

When the action finishes at half time and full time you may be expected to provide a brief summary, using the notes you have scribbled in your notebook, and ending with the score, so that the studio know you are finished. Then you will be off to do the post-match interviews (see below). But your job may not be over yet. Material will be needed for the following day's bulletins, which need to be written and recorded, with fresh material from your interviews.

Television

Many of the things already said about radio commentary, especially the need for thorough pre-event research and preparation, apply equally to television. Viewers can see if the commentator gets something wrong. And because sporting events are often viewed collectively, in pubs and bars, they are more likely to point out errors and air their criticisms, which may also be shared on social media sites.

But because television viewers can see the action taking place before them, commentary serves a slightly different function. The action will speak for itself. The commentator is there to put it into context, by naming the players on the ball or providing background information that will increase the audience's understanding. A good rule of thumb is to say less and let the pictures talk more.

Commentary will begin as the teams come out, with a short set-piece introduction. The company you are working for will have bought the rights to the event, so you will have access to information such as team selection and line-ups before any of the other media. Because this is television, key information such as teams and line-ups will be shown as graphics, and your script should take account of these. Again, the director will need to know the OUTWORDS of your introduction so that graphics can be screened at the appropriate time.

Although television commentators usually have a summariser sitting alongside them, they will be part of a much bigger team. The pictures they are talking to are controlled by a director in a truck outside the ground, who has access to a wide range of camera angles. Television commentators must cope with constant chatter in their ears from the truck. This can be distracting, but it will also be helpful with such things as statistics and player recognition. You will also be given advance warning and appropriate information if the director decides to cut to a celebrity in the crowd. You will have a monitor in front of you showing the pictures viewers can see at home, and you should comment on what is on the screen, while keeping one eye on wider events on the field. You can also ask the director to screen a particular shot if there is an important point you wish to make. Everything you say should add to what is already there. If it doesn't, say nothing,

The best way to study commentary is to listen to professional commentators, analyse their performances and try to copy those which work best. There is time to develop your own distinctive style after you have learned to do it well by imitating the best.

DANGERS OF LIVE BROADCASTS

Live and instantaneous coverage of sporting events imposes special responsibilities on the journalists and summarisers involved. Print journalists, even when working to the tightest of deadlines, have a little time to think about the effects of what they are writing, but radio or television commentators may have only a split second. Sporting events have strong potential for controversial or difficult moments, off the field as well as on it: crowd violence, racist chants, the appearance of streakers, serious injuries to competitors and even, in the most extreme cases, disasters like those at Hillsborough football stadium in Sheffield when nearly a hundred spectators were crushed to death, or the fatal fire at Bradford City soccer ground. Journalists reporting live must always be aware that friends and relatives of those involved will be watching and listening.

EXERCISE

Now watch the broadcast for which you have done your preparation. If possible, get a fellow-student to act as summariser. Watch it with the sound turned off, giving your own commentary on the action. Record the coverage and watch it again, this time with the sound turned on. Look out for ways in which the professional commentary differs from your own.

POST-MATCH INTERVIEWS

Because post-event interviews have to be fitted into a tight broadcasting schedule, they must be arranged before the event and interviewees must know precisely when and where they will be interviewed. Most major sports stadiums have a routine for post-event interviews, with a dedicated interview room, or facilities to conduct interviews in the tunnel leading from the dressing rooms to the arena, or at the side of the pitch. There will also be a sequence in which coaches or players speak to the media – usually television, followed by radio, followed by print media.

It is important to think about what you need from a post-match interview. It may simply be an overview of the key incidents in the game from each of the coaches for use in a highlights show. But you may also need material you can use in bulletins the following day, so you will need to ask questions about injuries to players, the consequences of sendings-off or bookings, and perhaps talk about the next fixture in the light of what has happened in the one you have just covered.

UPDATE REPORTING

Radio or television stations not providing commentary on an event may choose to send a reporter to provide a series of brief updates, often into a round-up programme which provides an overview of all the sporting action which is taking place at that time. This will typically involve the reporter in providing a short preview, followed by updates either at predetermined times or when something of significance happens, such as a goal at a soccer match. Summaries will also be expected at half time and full time. The time allotted to the reporter may be as little as 10–20 seconds (60 words maximum) so, again, the ability to write concisely is paramount. Outwords will normally be the scoreline.

Example

Victor Wanyama has given Celtic the lead here in Glasgow, rising above the Barcelona defence to head home from close range. It was very much against the run of play, with Messi scooping the ball over the bar and Sanchez having a penalty appeal turned down. But it's Celtic 1, Barcelona 0.

Summary

Sports journalists working in broadcasting share many of the objectives of their colleagues working in print, and must approach their tasks with the same commitment to thorough research and an equal depth of background knowledge. They must also be able to make full use of the additional tools that broadcasting offers them. Successful broadcast sports journalists must master the more complex language at their disposal and be able to handle the range of formats in which sports news is covered on radio and television. And they must acquire the performance skills needed to put over information successfully in sound and vision.

10 Online journalism

Chapter Summary

- The importance of online journalism
- Modes of online content
- Online writing style and presentation
- Search engine optimisation (SEO)
- Interactivity and social media
- Live, minute-by-minute reporting
- Blogs, podcasts and webchats

Learning Objectives

- To be aware of the challenges and opportunities offered by online journalism
- To understand how online journalism uses and adapts the skills of print and broadcast journalism
- To be aware of the unique and innovative features of online journalism and to understand both its advantages and constraints
- To be able to write, adapt and present material for the web
- To understand the principles of live online reporting

The most important developments in sports journalism in recent years have been the growth of ONLINE reporting via websites and social media sites, and the ability of fans to access them wherever they are, from an ever-growing range of mobile devices. This in turn has created an appetite for instant news, match reports, analysis and comment, and sports journalists have adapted the ways in which they work to meet this demand.

For many people, websites and social media sites are now the first, and sometimes the only, sources to which they turn when they want sports information. They like the speed, instant accessibility and interactivity they offer. As the number of websites has proliferated, so the competition between them has become fiercer, and media organisations now depend more on the revenues popular websites can bring in. Many breaking stories now appear first on social media sites, where they are quickly picked up and developed by other journalists, and serve as 'tasters' for fuller stories on websites and print or broadcast media. Website journalists have developed ways of grabbing and retaining the attention of their audiences by offering breaking news and minute-by-minute live reports of sports events, provided in the entertaining and irreverent style familiar to the young and tech-savvy who turn to them for their fix of sport. Schedules, results, statistics, tweets from writers, alerts warning subscribers when an event is about to begin, e-mails of breaking news, and video delivered direct to smartphones – these are all part of the online package. And no longer is the flow of information one-way. Online journalism is interactive, a two-way process, a conversation between readers and journalists, who encourage texts, e-mails and tweets to keep consumers involved. They provide another way of holding an audience. They can also be used to gauge reader reaction to your work and can be a source of follow-ups for journalists. But it is important that such contributions are carefully monitored for abusive, racist, bigoted, sexist or offensive material, and it is always possible to remove the comment facility if necessary on certain stories.

THE IMPORTANCE OF ONLINE JOURNALISM

The development of digital communication means that journalism is no longer the preserve of professional journalists working for corporate media organisations. The internet has given everybody the opportunity to become a reporter – to post stories and pictures on websites or distribute them via social media, to interact with journalists, to blog and comment about the stories of the day. This is a good thing in many ways, and opens up a range of additional sources for professional journalists. But it also means that there is a lot of poor quality and ill-informed material online, at best badly written, opinionated and self-indulgent, at worst, passing off rumour and untruth as fact.

The best online journalism requires the disciplined, professional approach and mastery of the core journalistic skills we have already looked at. But it also offers fresh challenges and opportunities to sports journalists, allowing them to hold on to and expand their audiences in an age of rapidly changing communication techniques. Online journalism can be experimental, innovative and collaborative, and journalists must be aware of the techniques and possibilities it offers. But it should start from sound journalistic principles, and add-ons such as audio, video, graphics and use of social media should enhance rather than distract from sound journalistic principles.

MODES OF ONLINE CONTENT

Social media as a journalistic platform

We have already seen in Chapter 4 how social media sites have become important sources of information for journalists. They have also become vital platforms for breaking stories, for getting a story out instantly to a host of followers hungry for the latest news about their favourite teams. Many journalists now put all their stories on Twitter first, keying in their 140 characters as they leave the press conference or the training ground. Social media sites offer individual journalists their own brands, virtually their own websites. Their followers will retweet such stories and they will appear, with the journalist credited, on fans' forums, ensuring a healthy audience. Many of that audience may then look for the story in full on the journalist's main platform, bringing in a more diverse audience. Local radio stations, for instance, traditionally attract older listeners, but are now picking up listeners among younger sports fans who have been alerted to stories on social media sites.

Using sites like Twitter, with its 140-character limit, emphasises the need for sports journalists to be able to write tightly and tell a story as concisely as possible. Broadcast journalists can also use social media sites as a platform for interview clips, placing audio on sites such as Audioboo. They can also broadcast live to Twitterfeed, where the material will be saved as a podcast. And social media sites can be a useful way for broadcasters to develop a big story before anyone becomes available for interview. Fans will certainly be talking about that story, and one way of doing a VOX POP without leaving the office is to follow the subject on social media sites. Fans will also sometimes come up with ideas or angles journalists have not thought of, and one way of involving them is to put out a request for questions before an interview, and use the good ones.

Fans expect sports journalists' social media comments to be lively and opinionated as well as factual, and this is a good thing. But a word of warning. The speed and informality of social media sites means that it is very easy to make a fool of yourself in an unguarded moment. Journalists should have more sense, and apply the same restraints to what they write on social media sites as they would to what they write for any other platform. Never say anything you wouldn't say on radio, television or a website.

New technology has changed the landscape dramatically for journalists. We can run stories immediately, get stories out there quickly. And it means you are able to own that story. It is retweeted by people, but can always be traced back to you. We also put stories from our bulletins on Twitter. It has widened our audience, who tended to belong to a certain demographic. And we can put stories out in advance of our bulletins, giving them greater immediacy. It also allows interactivity with our listeners. If we want reaction to a story, we can get it immediately.

Paul Walker, sports editor, BBC Radio Sheffield

Websites

The best websites tend to be those run by established media organisations and staffed by trained, professional journalists. Consequently, those which grew out of print-based organisations began by simply making the content of the printed version, including headlines and pictures, available online. This is called REPURPOSING or SHOVELLING content. Many newspaper-based websites still do this.

But many have also embraced the new opportunities the web has made available. They have developed journalism which takes the content of the printed story and combines it with new content from other sources, such as pictures and captions, audio or video, graphics, and links to ARCHIVE stories or other sites (see the Michael Phelps story below). This is known as RECOMBINING. It also involves making stories more user-friendly by breaking them up with CROSSHEADS and using bullet points, quote boxes or summaries. But don't overdo it, or it becomes distracting for the user.

Another approach is REWRITING – taking print content and rewriting it and/or abbreviating it for the web.

Finally, of course, there is content developed primarily or exclusively for websites. Examples of this are the live, minute-by-minute reports of sports events outlined below.

Most newspaper-based websites contain a combination of all four of these modes.

ONLINE WRITING STYLE

There is no limit to the amount of space available on a website, but that does not give journalists licence to write loosely and at length. In fact, the opposite is true. People look to websites to provide the information they are seeking quickly and easily. It therefore needs to be short, sharp and to the point.

People tend to scan the internet, looking for specific information, which they want to take in quickly. Online journalists must make this easy by writing simply. They must also bear in mind that website users, unlike the readers of national newspapers, often come from a wide range of educational backgrounds, and all of them need to be able to understand what they are reading with minimal effort. Clever, florid writing, no matter how stylish, is not the way to do that. The style required is similar to that used by tabloid journalists – short, simple sentences, short, familiar words.

Search engine optimisation

It must also be remembered that most people will come across what you have written not by turning a page, but by searching deliberately for the content either within the site or by using a global search engine such as Google. It is therefore vital that those search engines find your material efficiently, which means that both story and headline should be written with SEARCH ENGINE OPTIMISATION (SEO) in mind. This means attempting to get your story to the top of the list of the many which may be found by the search engine, because it is the ones at the top which are more likely to be read.

This is especially important with headlines, which are shorter online than in print, so they can quickly be scanned. An online headline should ideally be no more than six words. It should include key words likely to be used by someone who is searching for that story, such as:

Leeds knock Chelsea out of Cup

It sums up the story succinctly and uses the three words – Leeds, Chelsea and Cup – users are most likely to use when searching for the story. There is no place for clever or cryptic headlines on a website. A useful tip is to write your headlines as though you were typing a search into Google, with key words to the left if possible.

Including information from the headline in the intro to the story will improve SEO still further, and writers should keep sentences tight and language simple and searchable throughout the rest of the story.

The bare bones of the story should be told in the first three paragraphs with background added in the fourth or fifth paragraphs to add context and explain why the story is important. If video or graphics are used, these too should be kept simple: a 30-second clip of a player or manager speaking is usually enough. For more complex content, add a link to YouTube or some other source, such as the BBC iPlayer.

Be careful, too, about dates in your stories. Unlike a newspaper, where a day's news is ranked by importance, on the web more weight is given to breaking stories simply because they are new, and it is the breaking stories which are most likely to appear on the home page. Many users will read those stories almost immediately, but they may remain on the site for ever and some people may not read them until days or weeks later. Writers should therefore avoid using words like 'this morning' or 'today', but instead give the precise date.

PRESENTATION

The shape of a computer screen (and the even smaller screens on the mobile devices now available), its relatively small size compared with a newspaper page, the availability of additional elements such as sound and video clips, and the need to allow users to navigate their way round the site dictate the way in which information is presented online. The roles occupied by page designers and sub-editors in print journalism take on even greater importance on websites. A web page can accommodate only a relatively small amount of information, so website users have to be directed simply and quickly to other pages where they can get the information they want. The task of the web designer is to get as much information as possible on a computer screen, without creating clutter and confusion. The space available for editorial content is limited not only by the size of the screen, but also because each page must contain navigational aids and sometimes advertising.

Editorial space takes second place to user-friendliness on a good website. Journalists therefore have to work within the constraints imposed on them by the site design. This often means finding new ways of presenting information so that it can be consumed easily on screen. Online journalists have combined some of the elements of print journalism, such as words, pictures, crossheads, bullet points and graphics, with elements from the broadcast media, such as SOUNDBITES and VIDEO CLIPS, to create a new form of journalism suited to a new medium.

A report which would appear in a newspaper as a single piece of copy may be split into a number of elements for a website. The basic facts will still be presented by means of a headline and paragraphs of copy, but background information may be displayed as FACTFILES in SIDEBARS, and quotes made available direct from the speaker by means of an audio or video clip.

Example

The following story was written for the sports pages of a newspaper. The italicised sections could be displayed as factfiles on a website.

Phelps swims into Olympic history

American swimmer Michael Phelps has become the greatest Olympian in history. He secured the two medals he needed at the Aquatics Centre in London to take his career total to 19 Olympic medals, beating the 48-year-old record of 18 held by former Soviet gymnast Larisa Latynina.

But he could only manage a silver – his second of these Games – in his signature 200 metres butterfly event and has signalled his intention to retire after the London Olympics.

It was winning gold as part of the United States 4x200m freestyle relay team which made Phelps the greatest-ever Olympian. *He also won eight gold medals in Beijing, to add to the six golds and two bronzes he won in Athens in 2004, though he failed to win a medal in his first Olympics in Sydney in 2000.*

The American victory brought the 17,000 crowd to its feet to salute Phelps' moment of history.

At 6ft 4ins tall, with a wingspan of 6ft 7 ins, size 14 feet and weighing in at 84kg, the Baltimore Bullet is the most powerful swimmer ever to dive into a pool. In addition to his Olympic successes, he has won 26 world titles and 37 world records.

His long-time coach Bob Bowman says of him: 'His greatest strength is his ability to relax, and focus under pressure. As the pressure gets higher, he performs better. At the critical moment, he is at his best.'

But the 27-year-old was unable to defend his butterfly title and become the first man in history to win three consecutive 200m butterfly titles.

Ahead at 150 metres, he was pipped at the final touch by the 20-year-old South African, Chad le Clos, who won by a mere 0.05sec. Four other swimmers were quicker than Phelps over the final length.

'The 200m fly didn't really go the way I wanted,' admitted Phelps. But of his record 19th medal he said: *'I had put my mind to doing something that no-one has ever done before. Nothing was going to stand in my way.'*

Latynina won six medals in Melbourne in 1956, six in Rome in 1960 and six in Tokyo in 1964 – a record that lasted for nearly half a century.

Next on the all-time list are Soviet gymnasts Nikolai Andrianov with 15 medals (seven gold, five silver, three bronze) and Boris Shakhlin with 13 (seven gold, four silver, two bronze).

Website version

This is how the same story might be presented on a website:

Phelps record 19th Olympic gold in relay

American swimmer Michael Phelps has become the greatest Olympian in history.

He secured the two medals he needed at the Aquatics Centre in London to take his career total to 19 Olympic medals, beating the 48-year-old record held by former Soviet gymnast Larisa Latynina.

But he could only manage a silver – his second of these Games – in his signature 200 metres butterfly event and has signalled his intention to retire after the London Olympics.

It was winning gold as part of the United States 4x200m freestyle relay team which made Phelps the greatest-ever Olympian. The American victory brought the 17,000 crowd to its feet to salute Phelps' moment of history.

But the 27-year-old was unable to defend his butterfly title and become the first man in history to win three consecutive 200m butterfly titles.

Ahead at 150 metres, he was pipped at the final touch by the 20-year-old South African, Chad le Clos, who won by a mere 0.05sec. Four other swimmers were quicker than Phelps over the final length.

'The 200m fly didn't really go the way I wanted,' admitted Phelps.

The quotes could be displayed as a separate story:

What they said

Michael Phelps on his record 19th medal: 'I had put my mind to doing something that no-one has ever done before. Nothing was going to stand in my way.'

Bob Bowman, Phelps' long-time coach: 'His greatest strength is his ability to relax, and focus under pressure. As the pressure gets higher, he performs better. At the critical moment, he is at his best.'

(Continued)

(Continued)

Sidebar 1

Phelps' Olympic record
London 2012 – 1 gold, 2 silver
Beijing 2008 – 8 gold
Athens 2004 – 6 gold, 2 bronze
Sydney 2000 – 0 medals
World titles: 26
World records: 37

Sidebar 2

His closest rivals
    Larisa Latynina (Soviet Union, gymnast) – 18 medals (nine gold, five silver, four bronze)
    Nikolai Andrianov (Soviet Union, gymnast) – 15 medals (seven gold, five silver, three bronze)
    Boris Shakhlin (Soviet Union, gymnast) – 13 medals (seven gold, four silver, two bronze)

FACTFILE
The Baltimore Bullet
Height: 6ft 4ins
Wingspan: 6ft 7ins
Feet: size 14
Weight: 84kg

In addition, the quotes (and coverage of Phelps' races and presentation ceremonies) could be carried as audio or video clips, or both.

All the information which has been italicised in the print version has been dealt with separately for the online version. Factfiles, because they display information concisely, can contain additional information to that covered in a single report.

Discussion

The headline is short and search-engine friendly, with key words *Phelps, record, Olympic, gold* and *relay*. His record can be presented as a graphic, with symbols in the appropriate colours for the medals, and his rivals' records can be presented in a similar way, and with photographs of them in action.

 **EXERCISE**

Select a news story, feature or profile from a newspaper and turn it into a piece suitable for a website. Make the headline suitable for SEO. Simplify the style, reduce the narrative to its essentials and present statistics and background information in a sidebar. Present quotes either in free-standing boxes or as audio clips. You may also need a separate section on what others have to say about the subject of the piece, and a picture-with-caption or video clip of the subject in action.

LIVE, MINUTE-BY-MINUTE REPORTING

One of the main advantages online journalism offers over other forms is that it eliminates the fixed news deadline. A website can be updated at any time, and the biggest attraction of online sports journalism for many fans is the ability to follow sports events live as they happen, wherever they are – on their computer screens, laptops, tablets or other mobile devices. The difference lies in speed of delivery and presentation. People want it now, and speed is more important than finesse. There is a lot of competition out there vying to be first with the story.

Sports reporting online is possible while an event is taking place, just as it is on radio and television. Indeed, some websites offer live commentary and even visual coverage, though restrictions over rights apply to online journalists just as they do in radio and television. However, all websites are free to provide regularly updated, running, written copy and still photographs of the action as it is happening, as well as considered reports when the event has finished. Websites can keep their users in touch with an event moment by moment by refreshing the site at regular intervals or whenever there is a noteworthy incident. With the various codes of football, for example, a site can be refreshed every minute or two, while tennis reports can be updated point by point or game by game, and cricket reports ball by ball or over by over. The important thing is to hold on to your audience by updating frequently. If nothing of interest is happening on the field of play, the gaps can be filled with background information, observations or analysis by the reporter, or by using the wealth of live comment put on to social media sites, often by people who are also in the stadium watching the action. Social media sites could have been invented for sports journalists with space to fill during an uneventful game.

The journalistic technique involved in live online reporting is similar to that employed by journalists working for evening sports papers. They file it from their laptops or dictate copy over open phone lines, often straight from their heads, whenever something significant happens. The difference is that in online reporting it is vital that the information arrives regularly, or you risk losing your audience to another site.

Style also assumes a much greater importance. Although your audience may span the entire age range and social spectrum, it is likely to be heavily dominated by the young and tech-savvy. Your content therefore needs to be youthful and bright and your tone blokey, if you are covering a sport followed mainly by young men. The best live online reports make the audience feel as if they are there (and many of them will be) by offering flashes of local colour – about the weather, or chants from the crowd, or the strip the teams are wearing, or the quality of the pies from the catering outlets – when the excitement on the pitch flags. Careful research of the teams or athletes is vital because this also provides the reporter with material with which to fill a dull moment, or embellish a notable contribution from one of the athletes. And you should always keep an eye on social media sites for comments from others who are watching the action, as the best of these can also be used to fill space and keep the flow of information coming.

Coverage should start well before the action begins, to capture your audience early. It should start with build-up material, with the team-sheets going online as soon as they are available. Your audience should be prompted when the teams come out on to the field, and you should give a clear signal when the match has started. Don't be afraid to signal important events, like a goal or touchdown, with a few exclamation marks!!!

Example: Live, minute-by-minute coverage

Liverpool v Manchester City
English Premier League
Kick off: 4pm

3pm Champions Manchester City have won their last seven league games in a row and are favourites to win today. Liverpool are currently bottom of the league. They are a side in transition, with new manager Brendan Rodgers anxious for success after a 3-0 defeat at West Brom on the opening day of the season. It kicks off at 4pm.

3.45 - team news: Liverpool will start off with the exciting 17-year-old Raheem Sterling: Reina, Kelly, Johnson, Coates, Skrtel, Lucas, Allen, Gerrard, Borini, Suarez, Sterling.Subs: Jones, Jose Enrique, Carroll, Henderson, Carragher, Shelvey, Downing.

Manchester City are at full strength and include Stefan Savic, who had a disastrous game at Anfield in the Carling Cup in January, on the bench: Hart, Zabaleta, Kolo Toure, Kompany, Kolarov, Milner, Yaya Toure, de Jong, Nasri, Tevez, Balotelli. Subs: Pantilimon, Lescott, Savic, Rodwell, Razak, Silva, Dzeko.

Referee: Andre Marriner (W Midlands)

The teams are out! As usual at Anfield, the speakers are playing *You'll Never Walk Alone* and there's a warm round of applause as the teams prepare to start the match. Liverpool will kick off - playing towards the Kop in the first half.

They're off! And what a start. Steven Gerrard gets in a shot after just 29 seconds, but it's well wide left.

2 min: Tevez makes space down the right, and gets the ball into the area, but it is cleared.

3 min: Johnson cuts in from the left, tackled by Kompany. The ball breaks to Gerrard, who shoots but is again off target.

5 min: Lucas, injured for much of last season, goes down with a knock to his right thigh. He can't continue and walks off, straight down the tunnel, in some pain. Shelvey comes on as sub.

6 min: They've started brightly, open, end-to-end stuff. And the crowd is making plenty of noise. If this keeps up, they'll be rewarded with a goal or two.

9 min: Balotelli spins round Skrtel, who drags him down. Will this be the first booking of the match?

10 min: The ref lets Skrtel off with a wag of the finger. He's lucky to get away with that. Kolarov blasts the 30 yard free kick straight into the arms of Liverpool keeper Reina.

And so on, but the key moments, when they arrive, are given some graphic drama...

34 min: GOAL!!! Liverpool 1-0 Manchester City. Gerrard whips a cross from the right into the six-yard area. Skrtel meets it at the left-hand post, and powers a header into the net. Anfield suddenly becomes a cauldron of noise.

HALF TIME: Liverpool 1-0 Manchester City. City started the brighter, but Liverpool have dominated the last 20 minutes and just about deserve their lead. But there's everything to play for, and the second half should be a cracker.

The second half would be reported in the same way, with a round-up and the reporter's analysis on the full-time whistle.

LIVE ROUNDUPS

Many websites provide live coverage not just from a single event, but from the entire afternoon's sporting calendar, in the manner of sports round-up programmes on radio and television. These will usually be collated by a journalist in the newsroom of the media organisation, using a variety of material coming in from reporters at events, from wire services and through social media sites. They will take a similar form to the minute-by-minute example above.

CONSIDERED REPORTS

Live coverage of an event will quickly be followed on many websites by considered reports similar to those we have looked at for print. These will concentrate on the important incidents in the short, simple, web-friendly style we have already looked at. Quotes from coaches or players can be added in the form of text as soon as they are available, or as video or audio clips. A headline (SEO friendly), picture and caption will be included, and links embedded into the text to take readers to other content on the site or elsewhere, such as archived reports involving the same teams, which may interest them. And to keep the site interactive and readers involved, space can be provided to allow them to add their comments and opinions to those of the reporter.

Example

Liverpool 2-2 Manchester City
Skrtel 34' HT 1-0 Y Toure 63'
Suarez 66' Tevez 80'

Skrtel blunder gifts City a draw at Liverpool

Martin Skrtel's wayward back pass straight to City's Carlos Tevez 10 minutes from the end denied Liverpool's new manager Brendan Rodgers his first Premier League victory.

Skrtel's powerful header had given Liverpool a half-time lead, but another defensive mix-up allowed Yaya Toure to scramble in the equaliser.

A Luis Suarez free-kick restored Liverpool's advantage before Skrtel handed City a reprieve and ruined Rodgers' afternoon.

But he will take encouragement from the fact that Liverpool looked much the better side. City were lucky to leave Anfield with a draw.

Particularly impressive was 17-year-old Raheem Sterling, who proved a handful for Kolo Toure. His side took a deserved lead after 34 minutes when Skrtel rose to meet Steven Gerrard's corner and head powerfully past City keeper Joe Hart.

City manager Roberto Mancini made a double change after the break. Jack Rodwell and Edin Dzeko replaced Samir Nasri and Mario Balotelli. It paid off at once when Toure turned the ball in from close range after Liverpool failed to deal with a Tevez cross.

But three minutes later Liverpool deservedly went back in front. Jack Rodwell was penalised for handling and Suarez curled a 25-yard free kick low into Hart's bottom left-hand corner.

Then Skrtel's fatal error allowed City to claim a draw.

The report would be accompanied by match statistics and video clips of both managers' comments from the post-match press conferences.

Discussion

The header provides the reader with a basic summary of the match – scoreline, half-time score, scorers and goal times. This would be followed by an action picture with caption and a headline. Note that the headline is written with search engine optimisation in mind. It contains the name of a key player and of both teams. The intro is also search-engine friendly, containing the names of both teams, two key players, the Liverpool manager and the Premier League. The body of the report summarises the key incidents and contains some analysis. Sentences are short and the language simple. It would be followed by other statistics – teams, substitutes, referee, attendance, and perhaps a detailed breakdown of shots on target, percentage possession by each team, and so on – and carried on the website directly above the live report of the match.

EXERCISE

Watch a live game on television. Carry out careful research beforehand into both teams, as you would if you were preparing to do a radio or television commentary. Write a three-sentence preview piece 10 minutes before the game begins. Provide the teams as soon as they are announced. From the kick-off, write a running report for a website, providing a short paragraph of one or two sentences every two minutes. Be prepared to fill gaps in the action with analysis, comment, colour, background or social media comment. Provide a three-sentence summary at half time and again at full time.

At the end of the match, write a short, considered report, concentrating only on the most important aspects. Follow this up with a separate piece containing after-match quotes.

BLOGGING, PODCASTING AND WEBCHATS

The internet has also opened up a number of additional ways in which sports journalists can communicate and interact with their audiences.

A BLOG (an abbreviation of WEB LOG) is essentially an online diary which can be regularly updated. You don't have to be a journalist to blog, of course, and the internet is teeming with blogs. But many of them are trivial or personal or ill-informed, and professional sports journalists have a huge advantage over amateur bloggers. They attend events in which many people are interested, they have access to the latest information and they can write entertainingly.

A blog gives a sports journalist the opportunity to develop ideas for which there is no space on his or her principal platform – more description or opinion or statistics. It also allows the journalist to develop a personality with whom readers can identify, and attract additional followers and build new audiences. The interactive possibilities of the web mean that the journalist can also invite readers to respond and take part in the debate – a useful way of building a loyal following.

Blogging style should be similar to any other kind of online writing – short, sharp and lively. The best blogs will attract followers because of the journalist's writing skill and expertise in his or her subject. Blogs take many forms and styles, and the best way to develop your own is to look at those which appear on respected sites by journalists you admire. Start by following their approach and you will soon develop your own voice and style.

A PODCAST (a combination of the words iPod and broadcast) allows journalists to talk directly to their audiences via a range of mobile devices. Sports journalists often chat about the latest issues, perhaps including interview clips or commentary, and the finished product can be downloaded by subscribers onto their mobile devices. Again, popular podcasts depend on the style, expertise and popularity of the journalists producing them. They often use music tracks to make them sound more interesting, and delivery style should be chatty and informal. An interview format, with a host talking to one or more guests – fellow journalists, sports people or celebrities – makes them quick and cheap to put together. A good podcast will concentrate on the topics of the day, be they big events or controversial stories.

A WEBCHAT allows sports journalists to hold online conversations with their audiences and answer users' questions via e-mail or text. Most of the best websites host webchats from time to time, usually involving their big-name sports journalists. The journalist will usually introduce the session by setting the scene – describing the subject to be discussed or, if he or she is at the venue of an event, describing the atmosphere. Again, the style should be chatty and informal. Presenters will ask for questions or comments, and then respond to them as they come in, using their expertise on the topic. Encouraging sports personalities to take part adds to the interest of a session. Try a few webchats out on various media sites to find the format and approach you find most successful.

Summary

The rapid growth of online journalism has prompted journalists to devise and adopt a new range of skills and techniques to cater for an audience that demand news, information, analysis and comment instantly, wherever they happen to be. These include breaking news, live, minute-by-minute event coverage, audio and video links, blogs, podcasts and webchats. Journalistic style has been adapted to the demands of the technology through which it is being consumed, and journalists have embraced the interactivity which digital technology offers, not least the ability to incorporate information and comment from their audiences.

Sports news agencies and freelancing

Chapter Summary

- The function of sports news agencies
- Profile of a major agency
- Their changing role in the digital age
- The place of agencies at major events
- The roles of freelance sports journalists
- A day in the life of a freelance

Learning Objectives

- To recognise the importance of sports news agencies
- To understand the skills required by agency journalists
- To be aware of the role of sports news agencies at major events such as the Olympic Games
- To recognise the roles of freelance journalists in sports coverage
- To be aware of the openings available to freelances, and the approach required to work successfully as a freelance

THE FUNCTION OF SPORTS NEWS AGENCIES

As we have seen in Chapter 4, media organisations have always relied on news agencies and wire services to provide them with sports news and reports that they are unable to source through their own staff or freelance journalists commissioned by them. National media outlets will never have enough staff to cover all of the sports and events that are of interest to their consumers within the countries they serve, and the increasing globalisation of sport has led to a growing demand for coverage beyond national boundaries. Similarly, regional and local media must rely on news agencies for their national and international sports coverage. The staff reductions which have been forced on media organisations by the fragmentation of outlets for sports content brought about by the digital revolution have made the roles of news agencies and wire services even more important.

Wire services provide a comprehensive rolling service of news, previews, fixtures, reports and results to their subscribers online. But the changing demands created by new media outlets means they have a growing role as processors of sports journalism, taking in material from a range of sources and preparing it for the specific needs of different platforms, from newspapers to websites.

The smaller news agencies, most of them based in big towns, continue to gather local news and sell it to national media outlets, but they, too, must now be prepared to provide material suitable for a range of media platforms.

PROFILE OF A MAJOR AGENCY - THE PRESS ASSOCIATION

The Press Association, based in the United Kingdom, is one of the biggest news agencies in the world. Its sports operation employs 70 full-time staff and many 'casual' workers who, like their counterparts in other media organisations, are brought in on busy occasions such as Saturday afternoons or weekday evenings when there are heavy sporting programmes. Duty editors, who oversee the agency's output on a day-to-day basis, and sub-editors, who process material as it comes in, are based at a purpose-built 'hub' in the centre of the country. Reporters are spread around the UK, and are responsible for coverage in their own areas. There is also a separate office which covers sport in Scotland.

The Press Association (PA, as it is known) was originally set up by the UK's regional newspapers to provide a service of both news and sports coverage from outside their own areas. Now the organisation's wire services, including the dedicated Sports Wire service, goes to all regional and national newspapers, and to all broadcasters, such as Sky, the BBC and ITV. Although the organisation covers all sports, its main day-to-day focus is on soccer and horse racing. In England, coverage is provided of all Premier League matches, there is comprehensive Championship (second tier) coverage, and some focus on Leagues One and Two (third and fourth tier of professional soccer). In Scotland, all Scottish Premier League matches are covered. In addition, the globalisation of the sport means that top division matches in Spain, France, Italy, Germany and Holland are also covered.

THE IMPACT OF THE DIGITAL AGE

Originally a text-based service, the digital revolution has seen journalists working for the agency adapting to the demands of new media outlets in what has been a rapid and continuing process. In 2007, none of the agency's reporters had received video training; by 2012, 80 per cent were video trained. They are now able to provide broadcast-quality video interviews from pre-event press conferences and other sources, which are packaged at the hub and sent to the organisation's digital customers for use on websites. The process will continue to evolve, moving into HD (high definition) and streaming material live from media conferences.

However, the rapid development of media platforms has also changed the way in which sports fans 'consume' sporting events, and therefore how agency journalists serve their needs. Until recently, the central activity of an agency reporter covering a sports fixture would be to provide running copy on the action, mainly for the use of the Saturday afternoon sports papers and the early editions of national newspapers. The increasing reach of satellite television and the growth of digital technology means sports fans are now more likely to consume the event live, either direct from a TV broadcast, or through minute-by-minute updates provided on websites or direct to mobile platforms. The agency reporter's task is now to add value to that live coverage, by providing supplementary material from the grounds, which fans can consume on their 'second screens', be they computers or mobile devices. Although they continue to provide pre-match scene-setters, team news from the ground and a match report on the final whistle, rolling reports are no longer produced. Now reporters blog from the grounds, using Twitter as a means of regular updates.

This material is collated at the hub, fed to subscribers, and blended with material on the event arriving from other sources. A minute-by-minute data service will be provided from major events by staff at the stadium, often ex-professional players, who provide a bland running commentary by telephone to a COPYTAKER. This will catalogue every goal, penalty, shot on or off target, free kick, corner kick, throw-in, foul, injury, substitution, booking and sending-off to satisfy the growing demand for sports data of all kinds. And because all major sports events are now televised, a journalist can watch the match on TV and report on it from the comfort of his or her desk at the hub. In the aftermath of the event, journalists will monitor social media sites for possible comments from those involved in key incidents, which can often provide the basis of fresh stories.

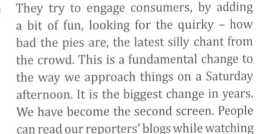

They try to engage consumers, by adding a bit of fun, looking for the quirky – how bad the pies are, the latest silly chant from the crowd. This is a fundamental change to the way we approach things on a Saturday afternoon. It is the biggest change in years. We have become the second screen. People can read our reporters' blogs while watching the game on TV.

Ashley Broadley, Sports Editor, the Press Association

THE PLACE OF AGENCIES AT MAJOR EVENTS

Agencies also play a key role in the coverage of major cyclical sporting events such as the Olympic Games. Few media outlets have the staff to cover all the action at multidisciplinary events such as these, or the expertise to provide authoritative coverage of minority sports. The gaps are filled by agency journalists, who can provide a rapid and reliable service of reports and pictures.

The Press Association had 90 staff at their base at the London 2012 Olympic Park, including reporters, sub-editors, photographers and data teams. They had a reporter at every sport. The journalists who covered them had been specialising in those sports for at least four years, since the previous Games in Beijing. They had spent much of that time getting to know the competitors, which made access to them at the Games much easier, and acquiring that sense of authority that goes with knowing a sport very well. Minority sports welcomed this media attention as a means of increasing the profiles of their sports. One journalist travelled to pre-Olympic events round the world with the British equestrian team. When the British team won gold, he was able to get an exclusive interview with the team's biggest celebrity, Zara Phillips, the grand-daughter of the Queen of England.

THE ROLES OF FREELANCE SPORTS JOURNALISTS

Because of the cyclical nature of professional sport, with peaks of activity at weekends and some midweek evenings, followed by troughs when little sport is taking place, many media outlets supplement their permanent staff with freelances. These are self-employed journalists who sell their services or their material to whoever will pay them. They may be hired to cover a specific event, such as a football match, because the media outlet does not have enough staff to send to all the games it wishes to cover; they may sell specific stories or features they have put together as a result of their own expertise; or they may be brought in to help out with the production of a programme, publication or website at busy times, such as CASUAL sub-editors on sports desks.

Many freelance journalists start as staff journalists and then decide to branch out on their own. They require the same skills as any other sports journalist, but to be successful as freelances they need to be able to operate in more than one medium (preferably print, broadcasting and online) and offer something staff journalists cannot provide. That may be detailed knowledge of a minority sport, or contacts who can provide a different angle on a story.

Specialising in a fringe sport can offer more work and a better income for a freelance than competing in the crowded world of mainstream sports journalism (although most specialists will be willing and able to turn their hands to mainstream sports reporting if the call from a sports desk comes through). As a cycling or sailing specialist, for instance, you will face less competition for work because few other journalists are experts in these sports. Demand for this sort of knowledge peaks during major events such as the Olympic Games, and that is when the media will seek you out. Outside those times, work may be available from the specialist publications that cover most sports. And many boost their incomes by doubling up on mainstream sports.

Ideally, freelances will establish themselves as staff journalists before specialising and branching out on their own. That way, they can make invaluable contacts on sports desks, build up reputations within the industry, discover their own strengths and weaknesses, and establish what gaps need filling and which niche sports are likely to be the most profitable.

> It might seem idyllic to be your own boss, but to make it work you have to be the toughest of bosses. You may find yourself working seven days a week, 15 hours a day one week, and have very little work the next. Freelancing can be feast or famine. You have to be prepared for hard work and be self-motivated. Unless you can be both, don't think about it.
>
> **Alan Biggs, freelance radio, television and print journalist**

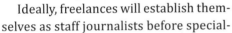

A DAY IN THE LIFE OF A FREELANCE

The news agenda changes quickly, in sport as in any other branch of the media. The first job of a freelance every day is to catch up with the latest developments – go through the websites of the major news organisations, or the clubs or sports you cover; listen to the radio over breakfast; read the newspapers. You have to know what is going on, and look for opportunities such as follow-ups to a breaking story. If a manager has been sacked, ask yourself who might replace him. You may have contacts among the candidates, or at the club. Give them a call. If you find a story, offer it to sports editors. You must develop a good relationship with sports editors because you are selling them something. Be principled: don't promise something you can't deliver. If you offered a story to an outlet exclusively, don't try to increase your income by sending it elsewhere. Your good reputation is your most valuable asset.

Researching, interviewing, writing or recording will take up much of the rest of the day. You will also need to go through the fixtures for the coming couple of weeks to pick out events you would like to cover. Speak to or e-mail sports editors to remind them of your availability. Yours will then be the first name that comes to mind when reporters are being allocated to those fixtures. Never assume that because you have worked for a person or organisation in the past, they will remember you and offer you more work. Freelances have to keep in people's faces. Never turn down work – but always ask how much you will be paid for it.

Freelance journalists have to make sure they get paid. Unlike staff journalists, they cannot expect a monthly pay cheque from which the right amount of tax has been deducted. They must have a system for keeping track of the work they have done and ensuring they get paid for it. This may mean phone calls or e-mails to chase up payment. And because they are self-employed, an accountant can save them money by keeping their financial affairs in order and making sure that claims which will offset tax are made. Accountants know about these things; journalists rarely do.

Then you may have a sporting event to cover in the evening. It could involve a two-hour drive, getting to the stadium two hours before the action begins, leaving it a couple of hours after the action ends, having interviewed coaches and players and filed your report, and getting home two hours later. It often means a 15-hour day.

Summary

Because sporting events tend to come in clusters, media organisations rarely have enough permanent staff to cover all of them at peak times. They fill the gaps by using material supplied by sports news agencies and by freelance sports journalists. Some freelances specialise in minority sports which staff journalists rarely have the contacts or background knowledge to cover authoritatively.

12

Sports public relations

Chapter Summary

- The work of sports public relations teams
- Media relations, websites and social media
- Players', managerial and staff public relations
- TV and video content
- Outreach work
- Major-events media operations teams

Learning Objectives

- To understand how sports public relations teams operate
- To recognise the value of social media sites to sports organisations
- To understand the skills involved in proactive and reactive public relations
- To appreciate the functions of major-events media operations teams

We have already looked in Chapter 4 at the ways in which the public relations staffs of sports clubs and organisations have for many years provided journalists with information and assistance to help them do their jobs. However, the arrival of the digital age and the growth in the range of media platforms, from websites to social media networks, now makes it much easier for them to communicate with their supporters and customers directly. No longer is sport totally dependent on the co-operation of the media to publicise its activities and promote its businesses. By setting up their own websites and making full use of social media sites such as Facebook and Twitter, many sports organisations have effectively become part of the sports media in their own right. And in order to service these outlets they, too, need the skills of sports journalists.

Although the majority of professional sports clubs still get by with just one or two people in their communications departments, the bigger ones, such as English Premier League soccer clubs and some American football, basketball and baseball clubs, have communications teams that run well into double figures – bigger than the staffs of many traditional media outlets. Indeed, as increased competition for the attention of sports followers has led to consolidation, closures and staff losses in traditional media, one of the fastest-growing areas of sports journalism in the first part of the twenty-first century has been in sports public relations.

THE WORK OF SPORTS PUBLIC RELATIONS TEAMS

While continuing to provide the media with the support described in Chapter 4, sports public relations teams have extended their activities to create their own media outlets. These now extend beyond the websites, which are the most important communications tools for even the smallest of sports organisations. The biggest clubs now have their own TV channels. But even the best public relations team will never have complete control over its organisation's image. In addition to their proactive work, they frequently have to be reactive, advising on the best way to deal with the fallout from the many negative stories generated in their high-profile industry. Players or coaches speak out of turn or behave badly; taxes are not paid; and sometimes *really* serious things happen: Sheffield Wednesday football club is still having to deal with the aftermath of the Hillsborough disaster nearly 30 years later. The sports PR's job is also to salvage reputations and protect the brand.

The activities of sports public relations professionals can be broken down into: media relations; websites and social media; players'; managerial and staff PR; television and video skills; and outreach work.

MEDIA RELATIONS

This is still one of the key roles of communications departments, as they are often known. It involves organising and hosting press conferences, from the weekly pre-match cross-examinations managers and coaches go through before each fixture, to photo-opportunities with new players or publicising the new season's kit. Press officers attend every home and away game, as well as reserve team games, to cater for the needs of the media.

On a match day, they will arrive at the stadium hours before the start of the event to oversee the running of the press area. This may involve troubleshooting if the ISDN lines journalists rely on are not working, directing journalists to the press room, providing information on players, dealing with requests to talk to players or the club chairman, looking after visitors from the opposing club, and organising radio, TV and press post-match interviews.

They will handle media inquiries on non-match days, provide background information for journalists at press conferences, and cover the events themselves for their own websites. On such occasions, the media may be provided with one player to speak to, while the club interviews a different one to give themselves an 'exclusive' on their website.

The growth of social media as a source of stories for journalists has led to an increase in calls from journalists who need to check the accuracy of stories which have appeared on social media sites. These calls would once have gone to managers or coaches; now media managers take those calls instead, to take the pressure off them.

WEBSITES AND SOCIAL MEDIA

The website is a sports organisation's main point of contact with its fans and often the first port of call for journalists seeking information about its activities. The commercial and public relations value of a good website is enormous, and its prime function is to promote the interests (often commercial) of a sport or a club. The editorial content may therefore be written more in accordance with principles of public relations than of independent and balanced journalism. Journalists should treat the material on them with the same care as a press release produced by any organisation seeking to maintain and improve its public image and commercial viability. Fans will go to them as their prime sources of information about the clubs they follow.

Such websites usually offer news stories, features, reports, press releases and statistical and historical information, but there is more to them than journalism. Their main function is often to sell merchandise or to promote other products, such as subscriptions to television and radio channels. But as with the older media, it is editorial content – the breaking news, the background features, etc. – which draws users to these sites. Some provide alternative angles on their own stories by reproducing what the media and others in the sport are saying on an issue.

But the growth of social media sites has provided a second, and often linked, outlet for direct communication with fans. Most major organisations also have a presence on such sites as Facebook or Twitter, and their followers run into thousands or even millions. These also carry links to websites, because the number of page impressions increases a site's revenue. Social media sites are also important in crisis communication, because it is there that the

> We put a lot of effort into social media, because it has changed the whole landscape of journalism. Fans are now grass-roots journalists. They originate stories and put them on message boards, where they are picked up by the mainstream media, and we as a club have to react to them. It is also a great communications tool for us, enabling us to speak direct to our audience.
>
> **Trevor Braithwait, Head of Communications, Sheffield Wednesday Football Club**

conversations between fans are taking place. Fans will often put stories they have picked up themselves – two players fighting in a pub, for instance – on social media sites or messsage boards, and they will often become the source of stories for journalists. It is vital, therefore, that the club's side of the story gets out there quickly, and many clubs will have someone covering social media sites full-time.

PLAYERS', MANAGERIAL AND STAFF PUBLIC RELATIONS

A major part of the job of maintaining a positive image for an organisation is making sure that individuals within that organisation get things right. So in addition to setting up interviews for players, coaches and Board members, advice will be given on how to behave with the media and what to say in certain circumstances. And when someone has said something ill-advised, which has been picked up by the media – a growing occupational hazard in the social media age – advice has to be given on how to rectify matters. PR skills are often needed to explain to fans why a certain player has been bought or sold, or why the manager has been sacked, especially if these decisions are unpopular.

Core journalistic skills are required to write match-day programme notes for the club chairman and the team manager, as well as a regular flow of articles on players. And in addition to the content of programmes, clubs also produce books and commercial brochures, and collate all newspaper and other media coverage for use by managers and coaches and for the archives.

TV AND VIDEO CONTENT

Television and video skills are also a vital part of the sports PR's toolkit. In addition to carrying out interviews with manager and players for their websites, most clubs film every home game. These are not only made available to their opponents, and used internally for record, analysis and training purposes: they can also contribute significantly to a club's income stream. Matches shown on their websites, either in their entirety or as highlights packages, generate hits from around the world. They are often available only to subscribers and can be a website's biggest revenue driver. Subscription packages may also contain material exclusive to the club, such as behind-the-scenes material and coverage of pre-season tours.

OUTREACH WORK

Like all large organisations, sports bodies need to promote their activities and reputations in the general community as well as with their fans. Ready access to sports celebrities makes this both easy and effective, and public relations teams are responsible for organising visits to children's hospitals, or to public service organisations like fire and ambulance stations and military bases – and making sure the media is there to cover them. Community liaison of this kind helps create a positive image of an organisation, well beyond its normal fan base.

MAJOR-EVENTS MEDIA OPERATIONS TEAMS

Some major international sporting events, such as the Olympic Games, are so large and so diverse that it is impossible for even the biggest media organisations to have journalists at every event. And providing a regular flow of results, quotes and information to huge numbers of media representatives – there were 5,600 journalists and photographers at the London Olympics – is a mammoth task. To achieve this, games organisers set up media operations teams whose function it is to gather results and information and make it available to the media. Organising committees may carry out this work themselves, or they may employ professional sports media companies such as Infostrada Sports. The media operations teams will be led by professionals, but most of the work is carried out by volunteers who are often journalism or media studies students, all of whom need the core sports journalism skills of researching, interviewing and writing.

Media operations teams begin their work months before the event, researching and writing official biographies on thousands of athletes – more than 10,000 in the run-up to London 2012. Most of the research is carried out on the web, and requires strong research, writing and interviewing skills, as well as a passion for sport. Athletes' biographies will prove invaluable to busy journalists both before and during the event.

Volunteers will normally be trained for their roles by attending several test events in the months running up to the major event, and attending at least one training day close to the start of the event. Their roles include staffing the media centre, which serves as a central base for journalists covering the event; organising press conferences and interviews and transporting athletes to media conference rooms; interviewing athletes trackside in the MIXED ZONE immediately after events to get FLASH QUOTES, writing them up and making them available to the worldwide media; and working in media areas at individual venues and stadiums.

Although volunteers are not normally paid, media operations work can be a good source of experience for aspiring sports journalists and an impressive addition to a CV.

Summary

One of the fastest-growing sectors in both sport and the media is in the field of sports public relations. Online media allow sports clubs and organisations to communicate directly with their customers via websites and social media.

(Continued)

(Continued)

They have effectively become media organisations in their own right, and employ sports journalists in order to communicate effectively and to get their messages across to the traditional media, who continue to provide an important link with their audiences.

Servicing the media is also vital to the success of major sports events such as the Olympic Games, for which few media organisations have sufficient staff to provide blanket coverage. The gaps at these events are filled by media operations teams, which provide results, quotes and statistics to the world's media. These teams are either recruited by the event organisers or by private companies set up for this purpose.

Appendix 1
Getting a job

While journalism is regarded by many as an exciting, even glamorous, occupation, the competition to get into it is intense. The expansion of the internet and the ever-growing number of websites has taken its toll on the print industry. Some newspapers have closed; others are shedding staff. But this has been offset by the growth of opportunities for sports journalists on websites, particularly at entry-level. Many websites are willing to give beginners a chance, writing blogs about their favourite clubs or minute-by-minute reports of events, often from television coverage rather than from the arena. Some of these opportunities are paid (though rarely substantially); others are not. Either way, they can offer invaluable experience which may help when applying for work elsewhere. But beware that you are not simply filling space for free for too long.

Full-time jobs are scarce, and employers are looking for people with qualifications and experience. Most media organisations receive far more applications for jobs than they can fill, and many would-be journalists are inevitably disappointed. But the media sector in most developed countries – and sports journalism in particular – has been expanding, and opportunities do arise for people with talent, enthusiasm and perseverance.

WHAT EMPLOYERS ARE LOOKING FOR

New entrants – whether they are journalists or photographers – normally have to start by learning the whole range of journalistic skills. That means they will be working as general news reporters or as part of a team of photographers. Employers will therefore expect applicants to demonstrate a wide range of interests, not merely in sport.

They will be looking for a good knowledge of current affairs, both national and local; an interest in people, places and events; the ability to write simple prose, with a sound understanding of grammar, spelling and punctuation; a willingness to work unsocial hours; calmness under pressure and an ability to meet deadlines; and the determination and persistence to track down a story. You will need to provide some evidence that you have the necessary talent, so use the internet as your publishing platform and your online CV.

CAREER PATHS

Most journalists start by getting jobs as trainees in newspapers, radio or television, or by enrolling on pre-entry training courses at colleges or universities. They are normally expected to work as general news reporters, and opportunities for sports journalism may be limited at first. It may be a couple of years before there is an opportunity to specialise in sport. Those who do make it to the sports department will often be asked to specialise in one or two sports, and to cover the affairs of one or more clubs. Many sports journalists stay with the same organisation all their working lives, but others progress from weekly to daily newspapers, and some cross over into broadcasting. Only the very best secure staff jobs on national or regional newspapers, or on national radio or television.

Broadcasting organisations may take new entrants direct into their sports departments. Many have their own training courses, or will demand recognised qualifications (see below).

TRAINING

In Britain, many journalists start by training on a local newspaper, under the terms of a training contract. There they receive on-the-job training with senior journalists, supplemented by BLOCK RELEASE to courses on which they can study for a professional qualification. Some of the bigger newspaper and broadcasting companies operate their own training schemes. Places on these schemes are sometimes advertised in newspapers and the trade press. Competition for these places is always very strong.

Many universities and colleges now run degree courses in journalism, some of which incorporate a professional qualification. Journalism schools have been in operation in the USA since the early twentieth century. It was the 1960s or later before they were established in Britain, where the National Council for the Training of Journalists (NCTJ) is the union and industry body which co-ordinates training. Many colleges train students for the NCTJ certificate, which is the standard journalism qualification in Britain. Entry to such courses may involve passing an aptitude test designed to establish whether potential students have the qualities necessary to become a successful journalist.

Minimum educational qualifications are usually required to gain employment as a journalist or entry to a training course. In Britain, the minimum job entry requirements are five GCSEs (General Certificate of Secondary Education) at A, B or C grades, or the equivalent. One of these should be English language. It is unusual, however, for entrants to be taken on without at least two Advanced-level GCSEs, and journalism is rapidly becoming a graduate profession. More than 60 per cent of recruits are now university graduates.

Some students on pre-entry training courses are sponsored by prospective employers, but the majority pay their own way. Many universities also offer post-graduate diplomas for students with a first degree who wish to acquire journalism skills. Courses normally cover the entire range of journalistic skills, including law, public affairs, and newspaper and broadcast journalism, though some offer options in sports journalism. They usually offer the opportunity to gain NCTJ qualifications or those of the BJTC (Broadcast Journalism Training Council) or magazine industry bodies. There are now a number of sports journalism courses on offer at British institutions such as Sheffield Hallam University.

Press photography courses are also available. These teach news values alongside photographic skills. Courses are also available in photo-journalism, which combines photography with reporting. As well as an interest in photography, the qualities required for acceptance on these courses are energy, commitment, personality, an enquiring mind and an eye for a 'different' picture. Some universities run courses in broadcast journalism, and there are college courses in magazine journalism which include news and feature writing, production and design.

For British college courses the minimum requirement is usually two A-level passes, though universities may ask for three passes at high grades. Most colleges only give places to people who have some work experience in the field and who are therefore sure that the job is the right one for them.

WORK EXPERIENCE

Getting a job, a traineeship or even a place on a journalism course is difficult, but your prospects will be enhanced if you can show a strong commitment to journalism. The best way to do that is by gaining as much work experience as possible on newspapers, in radio or television, or on a website.

To get a work experience placement you should write to or e-mail a number of local newspapers or broadcasting organisations explaining why you want to become a journalist or press photographer, what qualities you think you would bring to the job, and asking if you can work in the newsroom for a few days. Applications for work experience reach their height in the summer months, and you may increase your chances of being offered a placement if you avoid June, July or August. You will not be paid, but getting a foot inside the newsroom door is the best way to make contacts and hear about any job opportunities that come along. Many jobs in journalism are not advertised, but go to people whose work an editor knows and can trust. Some editors will take on – or at least publish the work of – people who are keen and good at the job, even if they have no formal qualifications.

The best way to get your name in front of employers who may be seeking to take on staff is to compile a portfolio of your work, or set up your own website or blog where you can showcase your work. In the end, employers are interested in what you can do. You may have to start small, by getting stories and features published in weekly newspapers, or in Saturday afternoon sports papers, which are often willing to take freelance pieces on minor sports to help fill their pages in advance of the day's big-game action. You may not be paid for them, but the cuttings in your portfolio will be invaluable.

Websites have provided thousands of new outlets for sports journalists, created many new jobs and offer new ways of satisfying the growing thirst for sporting inform-ation. Because websites are easy to set up and relatively cheap to service and maintain, they now hugely outnumber traditional media outlets. Almost every sports club and governing body has its own site, many of them employing professional journalists. The web supports sites operated by everyone from commercial and public service media organisations, through sporting organisations and individual athletes, to fans. Not sur-prisingly, the quality of sporting websites is equally variable. Some websites actively seek contributions from students, and may even pay a little, but beware of those which are simply trying to fill space for free. They can, however, provide a useful shop window for your work.

FREELANCING

As we have seen in Chapter 11, the busier days in the sporting week, coupled with reducing numbers of permanent journalistic staff at many media organisations and the needs of the growing number of websites which cover sport, means that there is a considerable demand for freelance sports journalists.

Despite this, freelance journalism is a crowded field, the work is irregular and rates of pay not especially good. Many freelance sports journalists supplement their incomes with other work. Many are also retired or redundant staff journalists, who are at an advantage because they are experienced and have very good contacts in the media industry. But there are opportunities for newcomers, particularly in the expanding field of online sports journalism.

Much freelance sports journalism involves reporting on or processing material from sporting events on busy days. But there are wider opportunities, and the most suc-cessful freelance journalists will provide a range of material, especially those covering minority sports.

Some freelances start by offering sports editors reports on minority sports or minor league matches in mainstream sports, and expand into news and profiles of players once their work is known and their judgement about what makes a good story or fea-ture is accepted. It may be necessary to persuade the sports editor that there is a lot of interest in your sport at that level. If you can become an expert in your own small field, the sports editor may start calling you, and once you have established the quality of your work, you may be offered bigger assignments, and eventually a job on the paper, broadcasting station or website.

It is a good idea to compile a portfolio of your work, even if it is unpaid work you have done for a local paper or website. When you have built up a small portfolio, you should compile a CV listing your qualifications and experience, and send it to as many sports editors as possible. Ask to go in and meet them. Get them to show you around and explain what they do. Enthusiasm counts for a lot with people who are looking to hire staff. Get your face known in as many newsrooms as you can. Most outlets do not need to advertise for freelance staff, but keep the details of likely candidates handy, so it is important to get your CV into as many places as possible.

Freelance experience can lead to a staff job for those who show enthusiasm and aptitude. But even if it does not, freelance experience with local newspapers or websites can lead to bigger things. National and regional newspapers employ few staff sports writers, but rely heavily on freelances to cover events at weekends and in the evenings. They are always looking for new writers, and will often be willing to give an opportunity to someone who can show a track record of producing competent work at local level. Local and specialist sport radio stations and television sports results services also provide opportunities for freelance sports journalists. In Britain, the BBC invites freelances to join its talent pool. News agencies such as the Press Association (see Chapter 11) and specialist sports news agencies employ freelances on a casual basis on busy sports days. Commercial agencies may ask a reporter to cover an event for several clients, which can be very hard work.

Freelancing has its advantages. You can work from home and you can turn down jobs if you feel like a day off – although if you do that too often, people will stop calling. It has its disadvantages, too. Some freelances work long hours because they cannot afford to turn work down. You also have to sell your work to sports editors, to chase up your fees and expenses from some employers, and you have no job security and no access to office politics.

But freelancing gives you the opportunity of working for more than one employer, and sometimes in more than one medium. Some freelances will cover an event for both radio (or television) and newspapers. Most large media organisations have their own freelance rates of pay. In Britain, the National Union of Journalists (NUJ) has a list of minimum freelance rates.

Whether they are freelances or staff writers, most sports writers specialise in one particular area. Only the top writers can cherry-pick across the world of sport. One fruitful area for freelances is to offer TIMELESS PIECES which can be used to fill space on the sports pages when there is little action to report. Another is the CROSSOVER PIECE, in which expertise in other areas is used to throw light on current issues in the world of sport. Examples include fashion (what the top sports people are wearing), business (the share prices of clubs, their merchandising activities, their problems with the tax authorities, clubs going into receivership), medicine (injuries to high-profile performers, the use of drugs), and celebrity reporting (the social lives of sports people).

USEFUL WEBSITES

www.journalism.co.uk – for jobs in journalism and tips for journalists
www.pressgazette.co.uk – more jobs
www.shu.ac.uk – details of sport journalism degree course
www.nctj.com – details of journalism and photographers' training courses in Britain, and qualifications available (including sports journalism qualification)

Appendix 2
Copyright

Journalists own the copyright in their own work unless they are directly employed by someone else to produce it. The copyright in an employee's creations is automatically assigned to the employer, but if work is commissioned from you as a freelance, you retain the copyright unless there is a contract to the contrary. Because you are self-employed it is your own, so make sure you don't sign it away.

All written work, sound recording, film and broadcast is protected by copyright. There is no copyright on ideas, but copyright protection in the UK and many other countries applies automatically if the work exists physically. This applies even if it is still in the form of a manuscript or computer program.

For work originating in the European Union, copyright lasts for 70 years after the death of the author of written, dramatic, musical or artistic work. Sound recordings, broadcasts and cable programmes are protected for 50 years. In other countries, the period is that granted by the country of origin of the work.

Copyright can be bought, sold or otherwise transferred, and copyright owners can license others to use their work while retaining ownership of the copyright. You should approach the copyright owner for permission to use material.

In certain circumstances, however, permission is not needed. Limited use of work is permitted for research, private study, criticism, review and reporting current events. Publication of excerpts, such as quotes, requires an acknowledgement.

Copyright applies on the internet as it does to paper. Material may not be posted on a website without consent. Many websites give details about how the material they contain may be used. Permission should always be obtained before establishing a link to another website.

USEFUL WEBSITES

www.intellectual-property.gov.uk – UK Patent Office
www.wipo.org – World Intellectual Property Organization

Appendix 3
Legal and ethical issues

JOURNALISTS AND THE LAW

Like all other journalists, those who specialise in sport must abide by the laws of the country in which they operate and in which their work is published or broadcast. Sports journalists will not find themselves constrained by legal considerations as often as crime correspondents or court reporters, but they cannot afford to be complacent about legal issues.

There will be occasions – when writing about sports people who have been accused of criminal offences or of drug misuse or some other misdemeanour, for instance – when a sports writer will need to be aware of the laws of defamation and contempt.

Defamation involves writing or broadcasting something you cannot prove which could expose the subject to hatred, ridicule or contempt, or the loss of business or professional standing. Sports people have been known to sue newspapers that have accused them of match-fixing, for instance. And don't forget that any quotes or interview clips you use from other people could be libellous. If you have any doubts at all, don't use them.

Contempt of court involves writing or broadcasting something which may unfairly influence court proceedings. For instance, the trials of the Leeds United footballers Lee Bowyer and Jonathan Woodgate were halted after a newspaper published an interview with a relative of the man they were alleged to have assaulted.

Sports journalists must also be aware of the laws of copyright and those covering data protection.

Of course, the law on these and other issues that affect journalists differs from country to country. For instance, laws on what you can publish before and during legal proceedings are less inhibiting in the USA than in Britain and many other countries. Even in the United Kingdom, the law in England and Wales is different from that in Scotland. It is not, therefore, possible to give detailed guidance here. Instead, you should make sure you are familiar with the law in the country in which you are working. In many countries, there are useful reference works written especially for journalists. In Britain, the main reference work is *McNae's Essential Law for Journalists*, edited by Mark Hanna and Mike Dodd (Oxford University Press, 21st edition, 2012).

The best way to avoid legal difficulties is to check all your facts scrupulously, and never make assumptions or jump to conclusions. If in doubt, consult the legal department of the organisation for which you are working.

ETHICS

In addition to legal constraints, sports journalists should also ensure that their behaviour and work conform to the ethical standards expected of all journalists. Most major print and broadcasting organisations, as well as media regulating bodies in many countries, have their own Codes of Conduct. Staff and contributors are expected to follow them, and they are often written into their terms of employment.

They deal with issues such as fairness, the correction of mistakes, dealing with people who are experiencing grief and trauma, offensive language, plagiarism, privacy, race and gender issues, the protection of sources and the use of subterfuge to gather information. They also deal with the personal conduct of journalists, such as conflicts of interest (when writing about a team you support or an athlete with whom you have a relationship, for instance) and the acceptance of payment or gifts from the people about whom you are writing.

You should study carefully the Code of Conduct of the organisation for whom you are working, or of one of the media regulating bodies in the country in which you are working. The Code of Practice of the British Press Complaints Commission (www.pcc.org.uk) is a useful statement of ethical behaviour for journalists.

You will find the following checklist useful in dealing with some of the ethical issues you may encounter as a sports journalist.

CHECKLIST

- Were the methods I used to gather my information honest, legal and transparent?
- Have I respected the privacy of the subject and others?
- If not, is my intrusion in the public interest? Why?
- Is my piece balanced, fair, honest, accurate and objective?
- Does it display prejudice because of race, gender, age or disability?
- Does it reinforce race or gender stereotypes or ageism or disabled issues?
- Could it cause distress to the subject or his or her family or friends?
- Have I been honest about my sources, even if I can't name them?
- Is the language I have used likely to offend a reasonable person?
- Have I infringed anyone's copyright?
- Have I reproduced anyone else's work without attribution?
- Has my objectivity been compromised by financial inducements or gifts?
- Are any photographs which have been digitally altered or enhanced clearly labelled as such?

Glossary

Actuality sound   natural sound effects, such as the roar of a crowd or galloping hooves, used in radio to help listeners picture the scene

Agent   a sports person's representative, who conducts wage negotiations and sponsorship and transfer deals. The agent may also speak on behalf of the athlete and deal with interview requests

Ambush interview   an interview conducted when subjects are approached in a public place or on their doorstep

Anchor   a presenter on a television or radio programme who reads reports and introduces items

Angle   the point of view from which a feature is written

Archive   previously used material which can be accessed via a website

As-live   a piece which appears to be live, even though it was shot some time earlier

Autocue   device which allows television bulletin presenters to read the text of scripts while looking into the camera lens

Block release   a period of time during which a trainee is released from his or her job to attend a training course

Blog (web log)   an online journal that is frequently updated

Breaking story   a story appearing for the first time

Byline   name of the journalist *by* whom a story has been written

Camera read   television news item without pictures, but with presenter in vision

Casual   a freelance sports journalist who is hired at busy times to supplement the permanent staff, such as a Saturday afternoon sub-editor on a sports desk

Catchline   name given to a piece of copy to distinguish it from others

Closed questions   questions which anticipate the answer or which are capable of being answered by a single word, for example: 'You must have been happy with your performance?'

Colour piece   a lively, descriptive piece, sometimes opinionated, funny or impression-istic, rather than a straight news report

Contact   someone willing to provide information to a journalist

Contacts book   list of contacts, with home and mobile telephone numbers and e-mail addresses

Copy   text of a story or feature produced by a journalist (from which a compositor once *copied* the printed version)

Copytaker   person who keys in copy telephoned in by journalists working away from the office

Copy item   radio news item read from script by the bulletin presenter

Copy tasting   assessing the relative value of a story and deciding its position on a page or bulletin

Crawler   moving text, usually along the top or bottom of the screen

Crosshead   a sub-heading, often a single word, in a newspaper column or other text, used to break up the text and make it easier to read

Crossover piece   feature on a general topic which uses a sports story as its 'peg'

Cue   short introduction to a radio bulletin item, read by the bulletin presenter

Cutaways   shots which allow an editor to move seamlessly from one sequence of action to another sequence which may have taken place much later in real time, for example, shots of the crowd or of coaches watching the action

Deadline   latest time by which copy should be received, or edition must go to press

Diary   contains information about events the sports desk may wish to cover

Direct quotations   the actual words used by the interviewee, enclosed in quotation marks, for example: 'I think I played very well this afternoon.' They are always in the present tense

Doughnut package   'topped and tailed' by the reporter from a relevant location

Edit points   points at which a tape editor needs to move from one part of the action to another, usually by using a cutaway

Embargo   a fixed time before which information supplied to journalists should not be published

Establishing shot   a shot of the interviewee, preferably involved in the sport he or she represents, shown immediately before a clip of the interview, to establish the person's identity in the viewers' minds

Estimate   same as Prospects (see below)

Exclusive   a story to which no other news organisation yet has access

Factfile   a column of facts accompanying a story

Fanzine   unofficial magazine giving a platform for the views of fans, who may also operate unofficial websites

Feature   a longer and more detailed piece of writing providing background information about people or events

Filing   sending copy from an event to the sports desk, usually by means of laptop computer, e-mail or telephone

Flash quotes   quotes obtained immediately after a sporting event, often by volunteers, for circulation to the media. Used at major events such as the Olympic Games, where media will not have enough of their own staff to cover every event

Follow-up   a story which expands on an earlier story

Freelance   self-employed, as opposed to staff, journalist. May have contracts with one or more media organisations

Hard copy   a story on paper rather than in a computer

Highlights   condensed version of a sporting event, focusing on the key moments

Intro   the first paragraph, or introduction, to a report or story, often providing a brief summary of what follows

Laptop   portable computer used by sports writers in the field, from which copy can be filed to the sports desk

Link   short introduction to a television bulletin item, read by the bulletin presenter

Live   a piece of television or radio filmed or broadcast as it happens

Log   a list of key moments, with the times at which they can be found on the tape

Mixed zone   area, often trackside, where media can speak to athletes after their events

NATSOF   natural sound on film (the television equivalent of actuality sound)

News access   agreement allowing television broadcasters who do not own the rights to use action clips on news programmes

OB (outside broadcast)   coverage (usually live) of a sporting event from the location at which it is taking place

Off the record   information which may help a journalist understand a story, but which is not for publication

On the record   information which can be published without restriction and attributed to the informant

Online   available via the internet

Open questions   questions which demand a considered answer and which cannot be answered with the words 'yes' or 'no', for example: 'How do you feel about your performance?'

Opinion piece   column expressing the writer's views on a controversial issue

Outro   opposite of 'Intro'; final paragraph which rounds off a piece

Outwords   the words with which a news item ends. Usually shown on written script to alert presenter that the piece is about to end

Package   television news item compiled by a reporter and consisting of several elements, such as voiceovers and clips of interviews

Payoff   *see* Outro

Peg   the basic event (often a news story) around which a feature is written

Piece to camera   a segment of television package delivered with the reporter in vision

Platform   medium by which journalism is disseminated, such as radio, television, website, newspaper or social media site

Podcast   recorded talk or discussion which can be downloaded from website

Press conference   a meeting called by an individual or organisation to provide journalists with information and allow them to ask questions

Press release   information provided by an individual or organisation to the media for publication

Profile   a biographical piece about an individual

Prospects   a list of stories and features that are expected to be available on a specific day

Recombining   taking the content of a printed story and combining it with new content from other sources, such as pictures and captions, audio or video, graphics, and links to archive stories or other sites

Reported speech   the interviewee's words are summarised by the reporter, with no quotation marks, for example: He said he thought he played very well. Reported speech is also known as an indirect quotation and is always in the past tense

Repurposing   making the content of a newspaper or other printed material, including headlines and pictures, available online. Same as Shovelling

Rewriting   taking print content and rewriting it and/or abbreviating it for the web

Running copy   story or report filed in a series of 'takes'

Running story   a story which develops over time and generates regular follow-up stories

Rushes   unedited tape of action, or of shots filmed for a documentary or a news item

SEO (search engine optimisation)   using key words to try to get a story to the top of the list on a search engine, as these are read first

Shovelling   making the content of a newspaper or other printed material, including headlines and pictures, available online. Same as Repurposing

Sidebar   a box alongside an online story containing additional information

Snaps   short news items sent out by agencies to alert subscribers to breaking stories

Soundbite   brief clip (usually between 10 and 30 seconds) from an interview for inclusion in a package

Standfirst   introductory paragraph which explains what the feature is about and usually includes the writer's byline

Steadicam   camera attached to the operator by a frame, which allows him or her to move easily and get close to the action

Stringer   freelance journalist hired by the day to cover specific events

Style book   guide to the organisation's preferred spelling, grammar and punctuation

Sub-editor   an office-based journalist who corrects factual, grammatical and spelling errors in reporters' copy, cuts or extends it to fill the space allocated and writes the headline

Summariser   'second voice' on broadcast commentary, often a current or former player or coach, who can add expert opinion on the coverage

Take   a segment of copy filed as part of a 'running story'

Timeless pieces   stories or features which can be used at any time to fill space when there is little live action to report

Two-way interview   dialogue between bulletin presenter and reporter

Unattributable   information which may be published, but not attributed publicly to the person who supplied it

Underlay   television news item read by bulletin presenter while appropriate pictures are screened

Upsound   as underlay (see above), followed by clip(s) of interview(s)

Video clip   a short extract from television coverage or an interview

Voiceover (v/o)   reporter's words over television pictures

Voicepiece   radio script read by reporter, but introduced by bulletin presenter

Vox pops   from the Latin *vox populi* (voice of the people), these are short interview clips with ordinary people, such as sports fans, which are used to add interest and variety to radio and television packages

Webchat   opportunity for a journalist to discuss issues and exchange views with an audience on a website via e-mail

Web log   *see* Blog

Website   online source of information about an individual or organisation; can be found by typing the name of club, athlete or governing body into a search engine such as Google, Yahoo or Lycos

Wires   copy provided to the media by news agencies, so called because it was originally sent by wire, although it has been available online since the 1980s. Most countries have their national wire services. In the United Kingdom most sports news is provided by the Press Association, though there are other specialist sports wire services

Bibliography

Adams, S. (2009) *Interviewing for Journalists*. London: Routledge.

Beaman, J. (2011) *Interviewing for Radio*. London: Routledge.

Boyle, R. (2006) *Sports Journalism: Contexts and Issues*. London: Sage.

Bradshaw, P. and Rohumaa, L. (2011) *The Online Journalism Handbook: Skills to Survive and Thrive in the Digital Age*. London: Pearson.

Cole, P. and Harcup, T. (2010) *Newspaper Journalism*. London: Sage.

Cushion, S. (2012) *Television Journalism*. London: Sage.

Farrington, N. et al. (2012) *Race, Racism and Sports Journalism*. London: Routledge.

Featherstone, S. and Pape, S. (2005) *Newspaper Journalism*. London: Sage.

Fleming, C. (2006) *Introduction to Journalism*. London: Sage.

Fleming, C. (2009) *The Radio Handbook*. London: Routledge.

Harcup, T. (2009) *Journalism: Principles and Practice*. London: Sage.

Hicks, W. (2008) *Writing for Journalists*. London: Routledge.

Hicks, W. (2013) *English for Journalists*. London: Routledge.

Hudson, G. and Rowlands, S. (2012) *The Broadcast Journalism Handbook*. London: Pearson.

Jones, J. and Salter, L. (2012) *Digital Journalism*. London: Sage.

Keeble, R. (ed.) (2005) *The Newspapers Handbook*. London: Routledge.

Keeble, R. (2008) *Ethics for Journalists*. London: Routledge.

Kolodzy, J. (2012) *Practising Convergence Journalism*. London: Routledge.

Lee-Wright, P., Phillips, A. and Witschge, T. (2012) *Changing Journalism*. London: Routledge.

Orlebar, J. (2011) *The Television Handbook*. London: Routledge.

Randall, D. (2011) *The Universal Journalist*. London: Pluto Press.

Starkey, G. and Crisell, A. (2010) *Radio Journalism*. London: Sage.

Steen, R. (2007) *Sports Journalism: A Multimedia Primer*. London: Routledge.

Stofer, K. et al. (2010) *Sports Journalism: An Introduction to Reporting and Writing*. Lanham, MD: Rowman and Littlefield.

Index